NAVIGATING NONFICTION

by Alice Boynton and Wiley Blevins

Credits appear on page 111 and 112 which constitute an extension of this copyright page.

ISBN-13 978-0-439-78291-3
ISBN-10 0-439-78291-0

2 3 4 5 6 7 8 9 10   40   14 15 16 17/0

Table of Contents

Reading Nonfiction

Nonfiction gives you information in many ways. There's the main article, of course. But there may also be added information in photos, captions, labels, and sidebars. Sometimes when you look at the page, there's so much stuff on it you don't know where to begin! Let's see how to navigate the page.

Step 1 **Preview the article to get set for what you will read.** The title, introduction, and the added information in the article below clearly show that you will read about a grasshopper.

Step 2 **Read the article.** The heading tells you that this grasshopper has a special, protective body.

Step 3 **Read the added information.** The photograph of the grasshopper helps you picture what it looks like. The caption tells you more facts.

Practice Your Skills!

1. Put an **X** on the pronunciation guide for the word *mandibles.*

2. Circle the caption that adds information about the thorny dragon grasshopper.

3. Why do you think the author gave this article the title "Cool Critters?"

PAIR SHARE How did you navigate the article?

Cool Critters

The thorny dragon grasshopper is found in the rain forests of Malaysia.

Imagine you've just settled down for an afternoon nap. Suddenly, you feel something creepy crawling up your arm. Its six legs scuttle across your shoulder to tickle your neck. Your hand whips around, ready to whap the pesky insect. BUT WAIT!

Are insects annoying pests or amazing creatures? Insects of all sorts do really cool things. So stop swatting and start reading to get the buzz on bugs!

Dressed for Protection

The thorny dragon grasshopper looks as though it's dressed for a costume party. But its beady eyes and thorny body actually help the grasshopper scare off **predators**, or enemies, like birds and bats. The swordlike points on this insect's body act as a caution sign to enemies: "Keep off!" If a predator ignores the warning, the grasshopper pulls out its next line of defense—its big overbite. Watch out! These teethlike chompers, called **mandibles** (MAN-duh-bulz), can draw blood!

Hip Hoppers

DO NOT EAT! Bright colors on the yellow-banded poison frog warn predators that these frogs are dangerous to eat.

Frogs are some of the world's most interesting creatures. Scientists believe frogs first appeared during the time of the dinosaurs, about 200 million years ago. How have frogs been able to survive for so long? The secret to their success is their ability to live in almost any environment on Earth.

Wild World of Frogs

Frogs are **amphibians** like toads and salamanders. An amphibian is a cold-blooded animal with a backbone that lives in water and breathes through gills until it develops lungs as an adult. Adult frogs can live in water, on land, in trees, or underground. Many live in more than one type of environment, hopping between water and land.

Many frogs have very special skin. Some frogs, like the Vietnamese mossy frog, use their skin as **camouflage**. This frog has bumpy, spotty skin that allows it to blend with its mossy environment. The more these frogs blend in, the more likely they are to survive.

Other frogs are easy to spot. Poison dart frogs have brightly colored skin that warns **predators** (PRED-uh-turz) to stay away. They ooze poison through their skin, which acts like a shield to prevent predators from eating the frogs. These frogs are so packed with poison that just one frog has enough poison to kill 20,000 mice.

Waxy monkey frogs do not hop or jump. They use their hands and feet to move along a branch, just like a monkey.

Hopping Helpers

These cool croakers can be a big help to humans. About 80 poison dart frog species live in Central and South America. Some scientists believe these frogs have chemicals in their skin that could someday be used to make **medicines** for humans to fight against pain and diseases like cancer.

Researchers are also studying frogs to learn more about pollution in the environment (see sidebar).

INSECT EATER. A blue poison dart frog sits on a leaf. This frog gets its poison by eating ants and beetles.

Frogs at Risk

The number of frogs living around the world has been declining for the past 50 years. Some frog species have even disappeared from the wild. Others have become deformed, or disfigured, developing with extra or missing legs, eyes, and toes. Deformed frogs have been found in 44 states since 1996.

What's harming the hoppers? Many scientists believe that habitat destruction, chemical pollution, and climate change are to blame.

Frog skin offers little protection against pollution, which can hurt frogs quickly. When researchers find many sick or deformed frogs in one area, that can be a big clue that the environment is unhealthy.

TOO MANY LEGS. A deformed leopard frog with extra legs sits on a human hand.

On Your Own

Read the article below about another animal with unusual characteristics. Then fill in the missing text features.

- Supply a title.
- Write an introduction.
- Write a description of a photo and a caption you'd like to include.

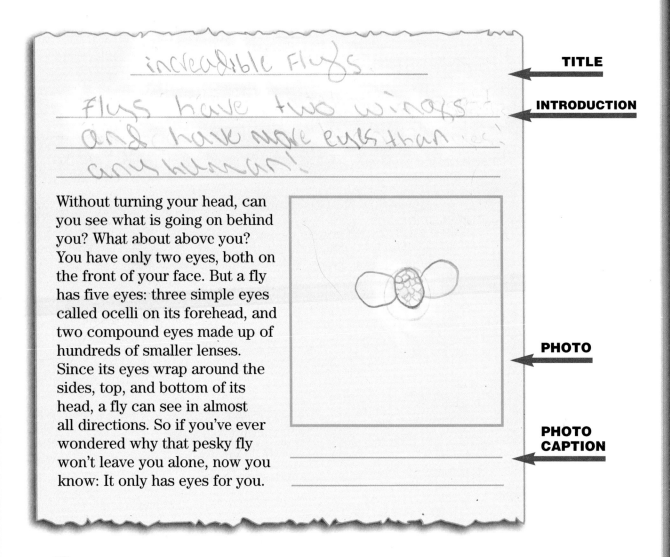

TITLE → increadible Flys

INTRODUCTION → Flys have two wings and have more eyes than any human!

Without turning your head, can you see what is going on behind you? What about above you? You have only two eyes, both on the front of your face. But a fly has five eyes: three simple eyes called ocelli on its forehead, and two compound eyes made up of hundreds of smaller lenses. Since its eyes wrap around the sides, top, and bottom of its head, a fly can see in almost all directions. So if you've ever wondered why that pesky fly won't leave you alone, now you know: It only has eyes for you.

PHOTO

PHOTO CAPTION

Think about other text features that could be added. For example, ask yourself, "Which word might need a pronunciation guide to help the reader know how to say the word?"

Reading Nonfiction

Here's how to navigate a page of nonfiction.

Step 1 **Preview the article to get set for what you will read.** The title, headings, and the map tell that you will read about our national parks.

Step 2 **Read the article.** This article is about ways to protect our national parks.

Step 3 **Read the added information.** The map shows where national parks are located.

Practice Your Skills!

1. Circle the introduction to the article.

2. Put an **X** on the heading in the article.

3. Underline the word that means "protectors of natural resources."

PAIR SHARE In which parts of the country are most of the National Parks located?

National Parks

Protecting Our Parks

The protection of wilderness areas dates from the time of Abraham Lincoln. **Conservationists** (protectors of natural resources) asked President Lincoln to protect the land around Yosemite (yo-SEM-uh-tee) Valley. On June 30, 1864, Lincoln signed the Yosemite Grant. It gave Yosemite Valley and the Mariposa Grove of Giant Sequoias (suh-KWOI-uhz) to the state of California. This grant became the foundation for all national and state parks.

Over time, the United States formed many national parks. It needed to create a service to manage all the land. In 1916, it developed the National Park Service. This service now covers a whopping 130,000 square miles, roughly twice the size of the state of Washington.

Glaciers, geysers, and grizzlies are just a few of the amazing sights you can encounter in the U.S. national park system.

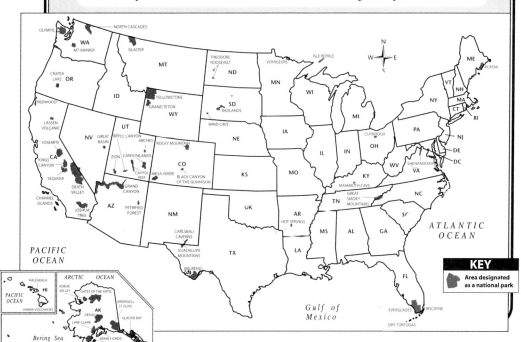

KEY
Area designated as a national park

Before You Read

Preview the article. Check (✔) the special features it has.

- ✔ title
- ✔ caption
- ✔ heading
- ✔ sidebar
- ___ map
- ✔ pronunciations
- ✔ introduction
- ✔ boldfaced words

As You Read

- Did you read the introduction before you read the main text? ☑ Yes ☐ No

- Did you read the information in the sidebar after the main text? ☑ Yes ☐ No

- Explain how you navigated the article. Futcher Children

After You Read

1. Why does the NCPA want to save the parks? Futcher Children

2. What kind of information did you learn from the sidebar?

PAIR SHARE What do the parks on the endangered list have in common?

Protect Our Parks

Our nation's national parks need some tender loving care.

Bison roam freely in Yellowstone, an endangered national park.

Be Nice to Nature

Ten national parks are on the National Parks Conservation Association's (NPCA) **most-endangered** list.

Problems facing the parks include building and road construction, **pollution** from power plants, and noise and air pollution from off-road vehicles (VEE-i-kuhlz) like Jet Skis, snowmobiles, and swamp buggies.

The NPCA hopes the list will alert lawmakers to problems the parks face. But conservationists say there are simple ways everyone can help protect the parks.

"The parks don't belong to us—they belong to kids who will be born in the future," says NPCA spokesperson Andrea Keller. "What will those kids see if we don't save the parks today?"

Most-Endangered Parks

1 Alaska's National Parks and Preserves
Diversity rules here. Icy glaciers, fiery volcanoes, and cool oceans grace these parks, which are home to animals as different as caribou and whales.
Threats: construction and oil exploration

2 Big Bend National Park, Texas
Big Bend is bat central. It is home to more kinds of bats, as well as birds and cacti (those prickly desert plants), than any other U.S. National Park. Mountain lions and black bears live here, too.
Threats: pollution and the draining of the Rio Grande for drinking water

3 Everglades National Park, Biscayne National Preserve, and Big Cypress National Preserve, Florida
The Everglades is the only place in the world where alligators and crocodiles live together. Wading birds, like great blue herons, and Florida panthers also live here.
Threats: pollution, tampering with water levels, and swamp buggies

4 Glacier National Park, Montana
Grizzly and black bears, coyotes, elk, moose, and mountain goats roam the forest, lakes, meadows, and high rocky peaks of this park.
Threats: building and road construction, mining, and timber harvesting

5 Great Smoky Mountains National Park, North Carolina and Tennessee
This is the salamander capital of the world. Thirty species of salamanders live in this preserved portion of the Appalachian (a-puh-LAY-shun) Mountains. Many other animals, including coyotes, bobcats, deer, bears, and bats, live here, also.
Threat: pollution from coal-fired power plants

On Your Own

Read the information in the article below. Then write a sidebar that gives information about Fire Island National Seashore. Look at the sidebar on page 8 to help you decide what facts to include.

Long Island, NY

Fire Island

Fire Island National Seashore in New York State preserves the island's beaches, dunes, maritime forests, and many marshes and bays. It is home to the piping plover, a bird that is endangered.

The Army Corps of Engineers is suggesting a beach re-sanding program along Fire Island to protect private homes built on the dunes. Experts believe that this construction will cause more beach erosion. It will also upset the nesting of the endangered piping plover, a local shore bird whose population the Park Service has been working for years to increase.

Fire Island National Seashore

(Location) National Seashore in New York.

The Fire Island National in New york preserves the islands beaches dunes, maritime forest, and many marshes bays.

It is home to the piping plover, birds that is endanger.

Threat: Experts believe that this construction will cause more beach erosion.

Text Structure

Description Ⓑ

Before You Read

Vocabulary Use the words to fill in the chart.

scarce   thermostat
tolerate   donor

Vocabulary Word	Related Words
thermostate	thermos thermometer thermal
scarce	scarcely scarcity
donat	donation donate
tolrate	tolerant tolerance tolerable

As You Read

Text Structure This article **describes** the changes in a bear's body and behavior during hibernation. To keep track of the changes, underline phrases that describe *hibernation*.

Text Features How do the text features help you understand the article?

After You Read

1. Describe how Dr. Barnes studies hibernating black bears.

2. Study the heading Making Headway. What does that phrase mean?

3. What additional facts did you learn from the sidebar?

A hibernating black bear peeks out of its den. Though they spend most of hibernation asle bears are often aware of their surroundings and can even open their eyes.

A Long Winter's Nap

Hibernating animals could someday help scientists save human lives.

Can you imagine sleeping through a season? Every winter, animals such as bears, squirrels, chipmunks, and raccoons hibernate (HIGH-bur-nate) in dark dens and nests. Now, scientists want to know their secret.

As the animals hibernate, their bodies slow down. But when they get up in the spring, they're ready to go—their bodies return to normal almost immediately.

Scientists want to find out exactly what happens to animals' bodies in order to find treatments for sick people, whose bodies have slowed down due to stroke or heart disease.

Sleeping Like Logs

Hibernation is a kind of deep sleep. Animals hibernate in caves, tree hollows, and underground holes or dens, to survive the winter when food is **scarce**.

Animals begin hibernation whenever it begins to get cold in their climate. For four to six months, they do not eat or exercise, and many do not pass waste. Their heartbeat, breathing, blood flow, and body temperature all drop to low levels. If the animals were not hibernating, they would be unable to **tolerate** these changes and would die.

Turning Down the Heat

Dr. Brian Barnes studies hibernating black bears at the University of Alaska. The bears hibernate in special padded boxes in a spruce forest on campus. Using surgically implanted transmitters—like mini radios—Barnes and his team measure the bears' heartbeat, breathing rate, body temperature, and brain waves. They also watch the bears with infrared (in-fruh-RED) cameras that see in the dark.

"The trick to hibernation is cooling," says Barnes. "When hibernating, bears turn down a sort of **thermostat** in their brains. Their body temperature drops, and instead of fighting it, like a human body would, they adjust" (a-JUST).

Dr. John Hallenbeck, a scientist who studies hibernating squirrels, finds that squirrels go through the same cooling-down process. "They become as cold as ice cubes," he says.

With cooler bodies, the bears and squirrels need less oxygen and blood flow, which makes it okay for them to breathe less and have slower heart rates.

If scientists could understand how the animals adjust, Barnes and Hallenbeck think they could learn to cool humans down when necessary, to keep them alive after a stroke or during heart surgery.

Making Headway

Studying hibernation has already helped humans. Scientists in Wisconsin found a way to preserve **donor organs**, such as livers and kidneys, for a longer time, thanks to hibernation research.

The Bear Facts

Bears' bodies go through some amazing changes during hibernation. Here are just a few.

Before going into hibernation, black bears spend weeks filling up on any food they can get their paws on. It is no wonder that during hibernation, they won't eat a bite!

heart rate: A hibernating bear's heartbeat drops from 60–90 beats per minute to 8–12 beats per minute.

breathing rate: The breathing rate drops from 6–10 breaths per minute to 5 breaths per minute.

body temperature: Temperature drops from 99–102 degrees Fahrenheit to 88–98 degrees Fahrenheit.

blood flow: Blood flow to the arteries drops dramatically in order to keep the head as warm as possible.

weight loss: Black bears lose more than 30 percent of their weight, plus 4 or more inches of fat, during hibernation.

waste: Bears do not pass any waste throughout the entire 4- to 6-month period of hibernation.

Other Heavy Sleepers

A baby gray squirrel snuggles up for a nap.

Many different kinds of animals hibernate to survive cold weather. Here are some that might surprise you.

mice • hedgehogs • skunks
anteaters • snakes • lizards
butterflies • slugs • snails
turtles • bats • frogs
crayfish • hummingbirds

Description

Reread "A Long Winter's Nap." Fill in the graphic organizer with details that describe each body change that happens during a bear's hibernation.

A Bear's Hibernation

The heart rate slows.

The Bears heart drops 60-90 bpm to 8-12 bpm

The breathing rate drops.

Drops from 6-10 breaths per min. to 5 breaths a min.

The blood flow drops.

Flows to the arteries in order to keep his head warm as possible

The body temperature drops.

99-102 degrees to 88-98 degrees

The bear loses weight.

30 percent and 4 plus

There is a change in its waste system.

Bears do not past any waist throughout the entire 4-6 month. period of hibernation

(Retell) Use the graphic organizer above to retell "A Long Winter's Nap" in your own words. Include as much information as you can remember.

Writing Frame

Use the information in your graphic organizer to fill in the writing frame.

Bears do something humans don't do. They hibernate.

They must hibernate because _food is scare in the_

winter.

Before they go into hibernation, they _fill up on food_

for many weeks .

Then _go into a cave for hibernation._ .

Some amazing changes happen to bears when they hibernate. These

include: _lose 30% of waite,_

body temp. drops 10 degrese, dont pass

waste .

These changes affect their _heart rate_ , their _body temp,_

their _waist_ , their _wait_ , their _blood flow_ ,

and their _breathing rate_ .

 Use the writing frame above as a model to write a description of the
changes in another animal during hibernation. Look in your science
textbook if you need facts that will help you fill in the frame.

Text Feature

Special Type

Take a look at a page of nonfiction and what do you see? There are words in **boldface,** in *italics,* and in parentheses ( ). There are words in different fonts, sizes, and even different colors. Why? To make them stand out, so you pay attention to them. They are clues to help you better understand the ideas in the text. Here's how to use them.

Step 1 The title is in big type, so you can't miss it. It tells what the article is about.

Step 2 The headings are boldfaced. They tell you the main idea of the text that follows.

Step 3 Pay attention to words in boldfaced type or *italics.*

Step 4 Use the pronunciation guides. They tell you how to say a word that may be unusual or difficult.

Practice Your Skills!

1. Put an **X** on the pronunciation guide for the word *Iditarod*.

2. Circle the boldfaced word that means "an event to remember something special."

3. Which is the accented syllable in the word *serum*? How can you tell?

PAIR SHARE What three important ideas do the title and headings tell you?

A Race Across Alaska

At 18 years and 12 days old, Ellie Claus is the youngest musher ever to run the Iditarod. She's a former Junior Iditarod champion.

Remembering the Past

The **Iditarod** (eye-DIT-uh-rod) is a sled-dog race that is held every year in Alaska. It is run on a trail that was originally a mail-supply route.

In 1925, part of the trail became a lifesaving highway for the children who lived in Nome, Alaska. The children were suffering from a deadly disease. A **serum** (SEER-uhm), a liquid used to prevent or cure a disease, had to be delivered to them—fast! The serum was transported successfully by a relay of dog-sled drivers, called *mushers,* and their dogs.

The Iditarod race is a **commemoration**, an event to remember something special, of that historic event.

The Race Today

The Iditarod is sometimes called "The Last Great Race on Earth." It begins in Anchorage, Alaska, during the first weekend in March and ends in Nome. Mushers have been running the race yearly since 1973.

Before You Read

Preview the article.
Check (✔) the special
features it has.

_____ title
_____ pronunciations
_____ headings
_____ introduction
_____ map
_____ captions
_____ photos
_____ boldfaced words

As You Read

• Did you read the
  title to find out the
  topic? ☑ Yes ❑ No

• Do you know what
  the boldfaced words
  mean? ☑ Yes ❑ No

• Did you use the
  pronunciations?
  ☑ Yes ❑ No

• Explain how you
  read the article. _and it by asking? to my_

After You Read

1. What is the name of
the communication
device that some
volunteers wear? _They where beepers_

2. Name some of the
services the volunteers
provide. _Save lives/rush ppl._

3. What examples
can you use to show
that the volunteers
are brave? _where it place dangerous_

PAIR SHARE Why are
the Dragon
Slayers important to
their community?

_to help
and save
lives_

Dragon Slayers: (from top, left to right) Falina Morris, 17, April Kameroff, 21, Karina Wooderson, 16, Erinn Marteney, 14, Patricia Yaska, Mariah Brown, Dione Turner, all 17, and Erica Kameroff, 16.

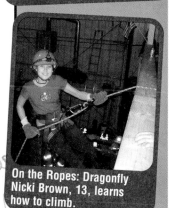

On the Ropes: Dragonfly Nicki Brown, 13, learns how to climb.

The northernmost parts of Alaska get no sunlight during much of the winter and get constant sunshine in warmer months.

Their Idea of Fun

An all-girl, teen team of volunteer firefighters is heating up its patch of Alaskan wilderness.

Aniak, Alaska, is a place unlike most others in the United States. About 600 people, most of whom are Yupik (YOO-pik) Eskimos, live in the **isolated** village, miles from anywhere. There are no roads running into, or out of, town. Many kids get to school on snowmobiles; student athletes travel to away games by plane. There are no malls in Aniak, not even a McDonald's. What do kids do to pass the time?

Life Savers

Some of them save lives. Aniak (AN-ee-ak) is home to the Dragon Slayers—an all-girl, teen team of **volunteer firefighters**. Dragon Slayers rush to the rescue in times of fire or medical **emergency**. Some wear beepers in school in case they have to leave for a daytime call.

Their duties take them far and wide. The Aniak Volunteer Fire Department—which includes a handful of adult volunteers—provides emergency medical services for an area the size of Maryland that includes 17 villages. That means that Dragon Slayers sometimes have had to take boats up foggy rivers to search for lost people. Some teen volunteers have even braved temperatures of 50 degrees below zero all night while on a search-and-rescue mission.

Teens Take Training

Amber Vaska, 13, is a Dragon Slayer-in-training, also known as a Dragonfly. If Amber were not a volunteer, she says, "I'd be really, really bored."

Amber and the other **recruits**, or new volunteers, go through a year of intensive training before sporting Dragon Slayer badges. They learn everything from how to take a person's pulse to the proper way to climb down a cliff using ropes.

Mariah Brown, 17, has been a Dragon Slayer throughout her teen years.

"I just like helping people," Mariah says. "When they come up to you, hug you, and say thank you, it's the best feeling you'll ever have."

On Your Own

Read the article below. Think about how the information in the article adds to what you already know about Alaska. Remember to:

- Read the title of the article.
- Look for boldfaced words.
- Notice pronunciation guides.
- Pay attention to graphic aids.

Denali National Park

Denali National Park and Preserve in Alaska is 6 million acres. It is larger than the State of Massachusetts.

Grizzly bear

The park was originally established to protect its large mammals. It is the **habitat** of large caribou (KAR-uh-boo), moose, and grizzly bears. Winter challenges these animals with **frigid** (FRIJ-id) temperatures of below zero and a lack of plant growth. Food is scarce. Grizzlies fatten up in the summer and remain in a deep sleep most of the winter.

Smaller mammals are also plentiful in this harsh, northern **environment**. In winter, ground squirrels and marmots **hibernate**, their body functions almost totally halted. Beavers and red squirrels hole up and survive on the food caches (KASH-ez) they've stored. Weasels, snowshoe hare, and ptarmigan (TAR-muh-gun), however, turn white and struggle to stay alive above ground.

Read the questions below. Put a ✔ in front of each question that can be answered by the article. Then, write another question about the article. When you're done, change papers with a partner. Answer each other's questions.

❏ 1. Which is the accented syllable in *ptarmigan*?

❏ 2. Which words are important to understanding the selection?

❏ 3. What kinds of plants grow in Denali National Park?

4. My Own Question _____

_____

Text Feature

Special Type

Each kind of special type is a clue to help you figure out the important words and ideas in the text. It's important to know how to use them.

Step 1 **You can't miss the title. It's usually big. Read it to find out the topic.** The title below tells the reader that the topic is snow monkeys. There is also a short introduction to the article.

Step 2 **The headings stand out. They tell you the main idea of the text that follows.** Each heading gets you ready for what you will read.

Step 3 **Look for boldfaced words or words in *italics*. They are important vocabulary about the topic.** Be sure you understand what the words mean.

Step 4 **Use the pronunciation guides.** The pronunciation for words that may be unfamiliar is in parentheses. The accented syllable is in capital letters.

Practice Your Skills!

1. Circle the boldfaced words.

2. Put an **X** on the word that tells which group snow monkeys belong to.

3. Underline the pronunciation guides.

PAIR SHARE What is the most important idea in this article?

Snow Monkeys

Brrr! Below-zero temperatures, howling winds, deep snow—winter can get pretty extreme. Now imagine being stuck outside without your warm winter gear. You'd scramble quickly, right? Yet some animals thrive outside in winter. How do they withstand the cold? They have special adaptations (AD-ap-TAY-shuns) that help keep them warm.

That's a Great Shape
Snow monkeys live in Northern Japan, where winter temperatures plummet as low as –9 degrees Fahrenheit (FA-run-hite). That's unusual because most **primates** (PRY-mates) live in the tropics where fruit grows all year. Like many animals living in cold regions, snow monkeys get by because of their shape. They have stocky bodies and short arms and legs.

Warming Up
The monkeys' compact and rounded shape means less **surface area** is exposed to the cold than those animals with long bodies and limbs. With less surface area exposed, less body heat is lost. If that isn't enough, they go swimming! These red-faced monkeys have been known to take dips into steaming-hot pools of water—just like humans might on a relaxing spa holiday.

Emperor Penguins

Emperor penguins spend the winter on the ice in Antarctica—Earth's southernmost landmass. They stay warm—at least part of the time—by huddling in a big group. They take turns braving the chilly wind and below-zero temperatures along the group's outskirts. Then they move into the group's center to warm up.

The birds also have layers of scale-like feathers to keep the wind out. On really frigid days, emperor penguins puff out their feathers. That traps air for even better **insulation** (in-suh-LAY-shun).

Emperor penguins are also plump. Up to a third of their weight can be **blubber**, a thick layer of fat. The blubber adds a layer of warmth and packs away needed energy for the times the birds don't feed, like when they're waiting for their chick to hatch.

Emperor penguins

Polar bears on the ice

Polar Bears

Polar bears love cold water and ice. Scientists have spotted them swimming 50 miles from land! In the Arctic Ocean, they ride huge chunks of floating ice and hunt for seals swimming below. So how do these 450-kilogram (1,000-pound) heavyweights keep from freezing? Part of the answer lies in the skin that's underneath their fur. Unlike the polar bear's fur, the skin is black in color. This dark color **absorbs**, or soaks up, heat from the sun, allowing the bear to stay cozy in the cold.

On Your Own

Here's an article about another animal that lives in a cold climate.
After you read the article, fill in the chart.

ARCTIC HARES Arctic hares can't talk, but if they could they'd tell you to wear your earmuffs. Like humans, animals lose some body heat through their ears. Why? A lot of it has to do with circulation. As warm blood circulates the body, it must travel through blood vessels in the ear. These vessels are close to the body's surface, which is in contact with cold air.

Unlike hares living in warmer climates, Arctic hares have short ears. This means that the blood has a short path to take through the vessels in the ears. The shorter the path, the less time the blood has to cool off. Now, that's an earful!

ARCTIC HARE

In column 1, write words you think should be boldfaced to show they are important to understanding the article. In column 2, write words that might need a pronunciation guide to help the reader. Use a dictionary to find the pronunciation for those words. Write the pronunciation guide in column 3.

① Boldfaced Words	② Words That Need a Pronunciation Guide	③ Pronunciation Guide

LESSON 6

Problem/Solution

Practice Your Skills!

Before You Read

Vocabulary Read the sentences below. Put a check mark in the correct box to show if the statement is true or false.

TRUE OR FALSE?

Cars that use a great deal of gas are **energy efficient**. ❑ True ☑ False

A **durable** house will stand for a long time. ☑ True ❑ False

Professional people have spent lots of time learning how to do their jobs. ☑ True ❑ False

A **shortage** of paper means that there is a lot of paper to use. ❑ True ☑ False

As You Read

Text Structure This article describes the **problems** four girls faced and how they **solved** these problems. To keep track, underline phrases that describe the problems. Circle the phrases that describe the solutions.

Text Feature How does the special type help you understand the article?

After You Read

1. Describe the housing problem on the Crow reservation. *Cramped/expensive in built*

2. Why did the girls think a straw house might solve the problem?

3. How did the girls convince people that straw-bale houses are safe?

BUILDING A DREAM: Lucretia, Kimberly, Omney, and Brenett working on the straw study hall with the help of volunteers.

Straw Dreams

To make a building out of straw was four girls' dream. Thanks to their knowledge of science, their dream recently came true.

Four Native American students from the Crow Reservation in Montana won a science prize for proving that buildings made of straw are safe and energy efficient. Then, they turned what had started out as a science project into an actual building for their reservation.

A WINNING IDEA

The four 10th-graders—Kimberly, Omney, Lucretia, and Brenett— entered their findings in a national science contest. They won first prize of $25,000.

When talk-show host Oprah Winfrey heard about the girls, she invited them to appear on her show and surprised them with another $25,000. She also gave them $20,000 worth of tools to help put their plan in action.

The girls used the money to build a study hall made of **straw bales,** bundles of straw that are tightly pressed and tied together. They chose to build a study hall because the nearest library is 12 miles away. With the help of 35 volunteers, they built the 900-square-foot study hall in just two-and-a-half weeks.

"I never thought I'd get to experience building a straw house," says Kimberly. "I learned a lot."

WHY STRAW?

After first hearing about the contest, which challenges students to use science to solve a problem in their community, the girls decided to find a solution to the reservation's housing problems.

Many families on the Crow Reservation live in overcrowded

①Houses were expencive to built/cramped
②They had heard about a woman who did it.
③did science experiments to prove it

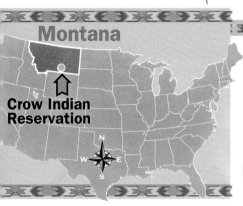

Montana

Crow Indian
Reservation

houses due to a housing shortage. On the Crow Reservation, as on many Native American reservations, two or more families often crowd into trailers or poorly constructed houses. These homes are not only small and cramped but are expensive to heat during the cold Montana winters.

The girls realized that straw houses might be a solution after hearing about a local woman who had built a house out of straw and **stucco** (STUK-oh), or cement for surfacing walls. The girls visited her home and found that it was really nice, didn't cost much money to build, and didn't require as much heat in the winter as most houses do.

"When you walk in, it seems like a regular house," explains Omney, "but then the walls are really thick, so it's warm and **soundproof**."

SAFETY TESTS

Although straw houses are cheap to build, many members of the Crow tribe worried that the houses would rot, or, more seriously, catch fire.

To prove that straw-bale construction is safe and **durable**, the girls built a model of a straw house, stacking straw bales and covering them with stucco. Then, they conducted science experiments.

To show that straw/stucco structures are **waterproof**, they hosed the exterior of the model house to see if any water leaked in. The model remained dry.

Then they tested to see if the model house was **fireproof** and **energy efficient** (EN-ir-jee ee-FISH-uhnt). "We put a blowtorch on one side of the wall and a thermometer on the other," said Kimberly. "We left the blowtorch on the wall for half an hour. During that time, the wall didn't catch fire, and the thermometer on the other side remained at the same temperature."

With the success of the project, some of the girls hope to build

CELEBRITY SCIENTISTS: (From left to right) Lucretia, Kimberly, Omney, Brenett, with Oprah Winfrey

straw-bale houses for their families. Kimberly enjoyed building the study hall so much that she wants to become a professional builder.

RAISING THE ROOF: Volunteers help build the straw-bale study hall on the Crow Reservation. The straw was later covered with stucco.

STURDY STRUCTURE: Volunteers stand in front of the completed study hall. Some of the girls have on traditional dresses.

Problem/Solution

Reread "Straw Dreams." Fill in the graphic organizer by describing the main problem in the article, how the girls tried to solve the problem, and the end result.

? **?** **?**
Problem

Attempted Solution

End Result

Retell Use the graphic organizer above to retell "Straw Dreams" in your own words. Include as much information as you can remember.

Writing Frame

Use the information in your graphic organizer to fill in the writing frame.

Four girls found a way to solve a problem in their community, the Crow

Reservation in Montana. The problem was that many families _____

_____

_____.

This problem happened because _____

_____.

The girls thought of a way to solve the problem. Their solution was _____

_____.

The girls proved that the houses would be _____

_____.

The girls not only helped their community, they won first prize in a science

contest, too.

Use the writing frame above as a model to write about the problem of conserving water in the Southwest and the steps being taken to solve the problem. Look in your social studies textbook if you need facts that will help you fill in the frame.

Charts

When you read about science, you will often see a chart that goes along with the text. A **chart** is a special graphic aid, set up like a table, that shows facts about a topic. For example, a chart can show how fast different animals can run or how much rain falls in one year in different U.S. cities. A chart organizes information in a way that makes it easier to understand.

Step 1 **Read the title to find out what the chart shows.** The chart below shows nutritional facts about one food serving.

Step 2 **Read the introduction. It tells you the main idea of the chart.** This introduction explains the purpose and value of food labels.

Step 3 **Read the headings on the columns.** The column headings tell us what type of information we will find in each column. The column labeled *% of Daily Values* tells what percent of a nutrient each food serving will give you.

Step 4 **Read the information in each row. If the chart has columns, read them from left to right.** The chart below shows there are 90 calories in this food.

Practice Your Skills!

1. Put an **X** on the title of the chart.

2. Circle the number that tells how many total carbohydrates the food contains.

3. How many servings of this food are in the container?

PAIR SHARE Would this be a good food to eat if you wanted to get more vitamin C in your diet? Why or why not?

What Goes on a Food Label?

A food label is an important chart that we use in our daily lives. All food labels must list everything that goes into making the food and keeping it fresh. Then you know if a food is healthful or not.

Nutrition Facts

Serving Size 1/2 cup (114g)
Servings per container 4

Amount Per Serving

Calories 90   Calories from Fat 30

	%Daily Values
Total Fat 3g	5%
Saturated Fat 0g	0%
Cholesterol 0mg	0%
Sodium 300mg	13%
Total Carbohydrates 13g	4%
Dietary Fiber 3g	12%
Sugars 3g	
Protein 3g	

Vitamin A	0%	Vitamin C	50%
Calcium	4%	Iron	4%

Percent Daily Values are based on a 2000 Calorie diet.

Calories per gram
Fat 5   •   Carbohydrates 4   •   Protein 4

Whether you enjoy swimming, biking, playing softball, or some other form of exercise, make some time to move your body.

Eating the right balance of fruits, vegetables, breads, and proteins (PRO-teenz) benefits your body in much the same way exercise does. **Nutrition** expert, Sheah Rarback, says kids today aren't eating as healthfully as they should be.

"They're overloading on sweets and fats, and they're not eating enough fruits and vegetables," she says.

Eating junk food instead of fruits, vegetables, and proteins keeps your body from getting the vitamins and minerals it needs to grow, develop, and be healthy. The good news is that eating healthfully is pretty easy.

"Start by choosing fruits or vegetables with dip as a snack," says Rarback. She also recommends trying a cereal with less sugar and asking your parents to switch from white to whole wheat bread.

After a few weeks of healthy eating and exercising, don't be surprised if you reach for an apple instead of a cookie and hop on your bike instead of plopping in front of the TV. Start moving, eat well, and get energized!

Vitamins to Keep You Strong and Healthy

VITAMIN	PROMOTES		FOUND IN
A	healthy eyes		leafy green vegetables, carrots, milk
B Group	energy		broccoli, milk, potatoes
C	protection against some diseases		citrus fruit and broccoli
D	strong bones and teeth		milk and fish

On Your Own

Read the paragraphs below. Then use the information to fill in the chart. In the last column, draw a picture of one of the foods containing that vitamin.

More Vitamins We Need

There are about 13 vitamins that are absolutely necessary for good health. In addition to the vitamins in "Eating for Energy," vitamin E and vitamin K are important for keeping your body healthy.

Vitamin E helps keep cell tissues healthy. Vitamin E is found in a wide variety of foods. Vegetable oils and whole grain cereals are good sources of vitamin E. Nuts and green leafy vegetables are also excellent sources of vitamin E.

Vitamin K is important because it helps blood to clot. It can be found in green and leafy vegetables, tomatoes, cauliflower, egg yolks, soybean oil, and any kind of liver.

Vitamin B6 is important for the brain and nerves to function normally. It is found in potatoes, bananas, nuts, red meat, poultry, fish, and eggs.

More Vitamins We Need		
VITAMIN	PROMOTES	FOUND IN

Charts

You'll see charts on the sports pages of newspapers, in magazines, and in ads. A **chart** is a special graphic aid that shows facts about a topic. A chart organizes the information and makes it easy to understand. It also lets you compare the information in the different categories.

Step 1 **Read the title to find out what the chart shows.** The chart below shows information about two U.S. states.

Step 2 **Read the introduction. It tells you the main idea of the chart.** This introduction explains what you will learn about these states from the chart.

Step 3 **Read the headings on the columns.** The column headings tell us what type of information about the state we will find in each column.

Step 4 **Read the information in each row from left to right.** The chart below lists facts about the state and shows the state's flower and bird.

Step 5 **Compare the information that is given.** For example, figure out the order in which states became part of the United States.

Practice Your Skills!

1. Circle each column heading.

2. Put an **X** on the nickname for Wyoming.

3. Underline the year that Rhode Island became a state.

 PAIR SHARE Why might each state have its own nickname? What does the nickname tell you about the state, its people, and its history?

STATE FACTS

Each state has a special nickname, motto, song, flower, and bird. These are selected to reflect each state's unique characteristics.

STATE	FACTS	FLOWER	BIRD
Providence ● **RHODE ISLAND** MOTTO **Hope**	DATE OF STATEHOOD **1790** NICKNAME **Ocean State** REGION **Northeast** SONG **"Rhode Island"**	**Violet**	**Rhode Island Red**
Cheyenne ● **WYOMING** MOTTO **Equal Rights**	DATE OF STATEHOOD **1890** NICKNAME **Equality State** REGION **West** SONG **"Wyoming"**	**Indian Paintbrush**	**Western Meadowlark**

Before You Read

Preview the article. Check (✔) the special features it has.

____ title
____ captions
____ column headings
____ photos
____ map
____ pronunciations
____ chart
____ boldfaced words

As You Read

- Did you read the chart title?
  ❏ Yes ❏ No

- Did you read each column heading?
  ❏ Yes ❏ No

- Did you find the boldfaced word that names the state?
  ❏ Yes ❏ No

- Explain how you read the chart.

After You Read

1. Why did people from many countries come to Hawaii?

2. In what region of the United States is Hawaii?

PAIR SHARE From reading the article and the chart, tell what you learned about Hawaii.

Coming to Hawaii

Settling in Hawaii

More than 2,000 years ago, people from the Polynesian Islands in the Pacific Ocean came to Hawaii. They were the first people to settle there.

Hundreds of years later, other people began to settle in Hawaii. They came for many reasons. Some Americans set up large sugar and pineapple farms. Many Chinese and Japanese immigrants came to Hawaii to work on farms. So did people from Portugal, Puerto Rico, and the Philippines.

Joining the United States

Americans wanted Hawaii to be a part of the United States. A group of American plantation owners made the queen of Hawaii give up her throne. Soon Hawaii became a U.S. territory. Hawaii became the fiftieth state in 1959.

Pineapples are still grown in Hawaii.

Queen Liliuokalani of Hawaii was forced to give up her throne.

THE 50TH STATE

STATE	FACTS	FLOWER	BIRD
HAWAII **Honolulu** MOTTO **The life of the land is perpetuated in righteousness.**	DATE OF STATEHOOD **1959** NICKNAME **The Aloha State** REGION **West** SONG **"Hawaii Ponoi"**	Yellow hibiscus	Hawaiian goose

On Your Own

Read the information below about West Virginia and Oregon. Use the information to complete the chart.

West Virginia

Charleston is the capital of West Virginia. West Virginia, in the southeastern region of our country, became a state in 1863. Some people call it the "Mountain State." Its state bird is the cardinal.

Oregon

Oregon, located in the western part of the United States, became a state in 1859. Its nickname is "Beaver State. The Western meadowlark is the state bird.

STATES IN THE UNITED STATES

STATE	DATE OF STATEHOOD	REGION	NICKNAME	STATE BIRD
Charleston West Virginia				
Salem Oregon				

 Add to the chart. Fill in the facts for your state or another state of your choice. Look in your social studies textbook for help.

Cause/Effect

Practice Your Skills!

Before You Read

Vocabulary Use the words to fill in the chart. Write each word under the category to which it belongs. You may wish to add some other words.

calorie	nutrients	stint
goal	fruits	confidence

Staying Healthy	
Food	**Exercise**
vitamins minerals vegetables	physical activity energize fitness

As You Read

Text Structure This article discusses the need for nutritious foods and exercise in order to stay healthy. To keep track of the **causes** of being overweight, underline the words that tell reasons for becoming overweight. Circle the **effects** of eating unhealthy foods and not getting enough exercise.

Text Feature How does the chart help you understand the article?

After You Read

1. What causes people to become overweight? *Eating unhealthy food & staying inside all day*

2. Study the chart. Which are the most popular and least popular fitness activities? In which two activities do the same number of people participate? *Tredmill, stationary walking & fitness walking & jogging*

3. Why do you think fitness walking is the most popular activity? Which activity is your favorite? *It doesn't take much work*

Have Fun! Get Healthy

It's time to get healthy! Start moving your body and eating the right foods!

Spring brings warmer days and delicious fruits and vegetables. That's why this is a perfect time for you to head outside to **exercise** and reach for something healthy to eat.

Unfortunately, recent studies show that many American kids are spending too much time sitting inside and eating **unhealthy** food. They're watching TV and playing video games while their bikes, sneakers, skateboards, and playgrounds go unused. And while a lot of these kids are sitting on the couch watching TV, they tend to munch on junk food. Does this sound like you?

So much sitting around and unhealthy snacking can cause health problems.

Move Your Body!

Exercise gives your heart a good workout by making it beat more quickly. Having a strong heart helps your body work more efficiently and makes you feel full of energy. Being in good physical shape also helps you to think clearly and fend off illnesses such as colds. Follow these fitness tips for a happy heart and mighty muscles.

- Go for a bike ride.
- Jump rope.
- Play tag.
- Shoot basketball hoops.
- Start up a softball or kickball game.
- Walk your dog.
- Get out the chalk and play hopscotch.
- Turn off the TV and go outside.

Underline = cause.
_ _ _ _ = effect

As a result of overeating and not getting enough exercise, today, 9 million American kids ages 6 to 19 are considered overweight. Being overweight puts kids at risk of developing serious health problems, such as heart disease and diabetes (DIE-uh-BEE-teez), later in life.

Balancing Act

Many people become overweight because their bodies take in more **calories** (from food and drinks) than they burn off through physical activity. You need to eat the right combination of **vitamins**, **minerals**, and **nutrients** to help your body work and grow. But beware: If you're thin, that does not necessarily mean you're fit. Health experts say that many American kids, including those who are not overweight, do not get enough exercise. In fact, one out of every five American kids participates in two or fewer stints of **physical activity** per week. According to scientists,

you should participate in some form of exercise every day to stay energized (EN-er-jizd) and to keep your heart strong. How many times a week do you exercise?

Get Physical!

Some fourth-graders in Idaho are following the fitness experts' advice. Students at Filer Elementary School in Filer, Idaho, will do a 50-mile group walk this month as part of the Big Walk, a school program that promotes physical fitness while teaching kids about Idaho history. Because Filer students want to be fit, they will walk 10 miles a day for five days in a row. Along the way, they will see many sights, such as the Oregon Trail, that are important to their state's history.

Follow in the Filer kids' footsteps by taking charge and getting active. As a result of giving your body the **fuel** and exercise it needs, you'll be able to think more clearly in school and feel better than ever!

How Americans Keep Fit

About 54 million Americans 6 years and older participate frequently (100 times or more) in fitness activities. This year their top activities, in millions of participants, are:

Type of Exercise	Number of People
Fitness Walking	17.2 Million
Free Weights	11.3 Million
Stationary Biking	9.4 Million
Running/Jogging	9.4 Million
Treadmill	7.0 Million
Resistance Machines	6.2 Million

Fuel Up With Good Food!

If you eat right, your body will thank you.

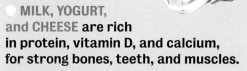

● **MEAT, FISH, EGGS, and BEANS** are great sources of *protein*, which builds body tissues, carries oxygen to the cells, and protects you from diseases.

● **MILK, YOGURT, and CHEESE** are rich in protein, vitamin D, and calcium, for strong bones, teeth, and muscles.

● **BROCCOLI, LEAFY GREENS, and TOMATOES** are packed with vitamins and minerals. You should eat five servings of fruits and vegetables a day.

● **BREADS, CEREAL, PASTA, AND GRAINS** are complex carbohydrates. These foods help you store energy, and you'll need a lot of energy while exercising!

● **CHECK OUT FOOD LABELS!** Some restaurants and school cafeterias now offer nutritional facts on the food they serve. Next time you get the chance, read the nutrition label on your favorite food. You may be surprised by what's in it!

Cause/Effect

Reread "Have Fun! Get Healthy!" Fill in the graphic organizer to show either the cause or the effect.

Cause

eating a lot of junk food

sitting around eating unhealthy snacks.

giving your body the fuel and exercise it needs

Effect

you get over weight and un healthy

risk of developing health problems

you'll be able to think more clearly.

Retell Use the graphic organizer above to retell "Have Fun! Get Healthy!" in your own words. Include as much information as you can remember.

Writing Frame

Use the information in your organizer to fill in the writing frame.

Because of _____

_____

_____, many kids today are overweight.

This can cause _____

_____

_____.

Therefore, it's important to _____

_____.

As a result, the students at _____

_____

_____.

 Use the writing frame above as a model to write a paragraph about staying healthy. Look in your science textbook if you need facts that will help you fill in the frame.

Time Lines

A **time line** is a kind of diagram that shows a series of real events and the dates on which they happened. The time line helps you make connections between the events. A time line can span large amounts of time. The information is always shown in time order from the earliest date to the latest date. Here's how to read a time line.

Step 1 **Read the title to find out the topic or period covered in the time line.** The title of the time line below tells that the time line will be about winter weather.

Step 2 **Find the starting and ending dates for the time line.** Some time lines are horizontal. You read them from left to right. Others, such as this one, are vertical. You read them from top to bottom.

Step 3 **Read the label for each date. It describes the event that took place.** The labels below give information about the unusual weather that happened in each year featured on the time line.

SNOWY WEATHER

1899 Blizzard conditions hit Florida, the farthest south snow has fallen in the United States up to this point.

1932 Two inches of snow falls in downtown Los Angeles.

1950 A storm known as "The Appalachian Storm" brings blizzard conditions on Thanksgiving Day. Up to 62 inches of snow falls in West Virginia.

1970 The largest hailstone ever documented falls in Kansas. It weighs more than $1\frac{1}{2}$ pounds and measures $5\frac{1}{2}$ inches across.

1977 Buffalo, New York, suffers through 40 straight days of snowfall. It is the first U.S. city to be declared a Federal Disaster Area due to snow.

1996 A January blizzard drops nearly 2 feet of snow on Washington, D.C. The whole federal government is shut down for a day.

2005 Cleveland has a record snowfall of 104 inches in the winter of 2004–2005.

2006 New York City's biggest snowstorm on record dumps 26.9 inches of snow.

BLIZZARDS HAVE LEFT A TRAIL OF DESTRUCTION THROUGH THE YEARS.

New York City, 1947, 26.4 inches of snow

Practice Your Skills!

1. Put an **X** on the date that shows when the largest hailstone fell.

2. Circle the words that tell the name of the city that was declared a Federal Disaster Area due to snow.

3. In what year was the Federal Government shut down for a day because of snow?

PAIR SHARE What examples show that the eastern part of the United States has had many large snowstorms?

Practice Your Skills!

Before You Read

Preview the article. Check (✔) the special features it has.

_____ title
_____ headings
_____ dates
_____ events
_____ map
_____ captions
_____ photos
_____ place names

As You Read

- Did you read the title to find out what the time line is about?
  ❏ Yes ❏ No

- Did you read the beginning and ending dates?
  ❏ Yes ❏ No

- Did you read each of the dates and the events in order?
  ❏ Yes ❏ No

- Explain how you read the time line.

After You Read

1. When was one of the first books about weather written?

2. In what year was the first weather satellite sent up?

PAIR SHARE Why is it important to have accurate weather forecasts?

WEATHER WATCH
Past & Present

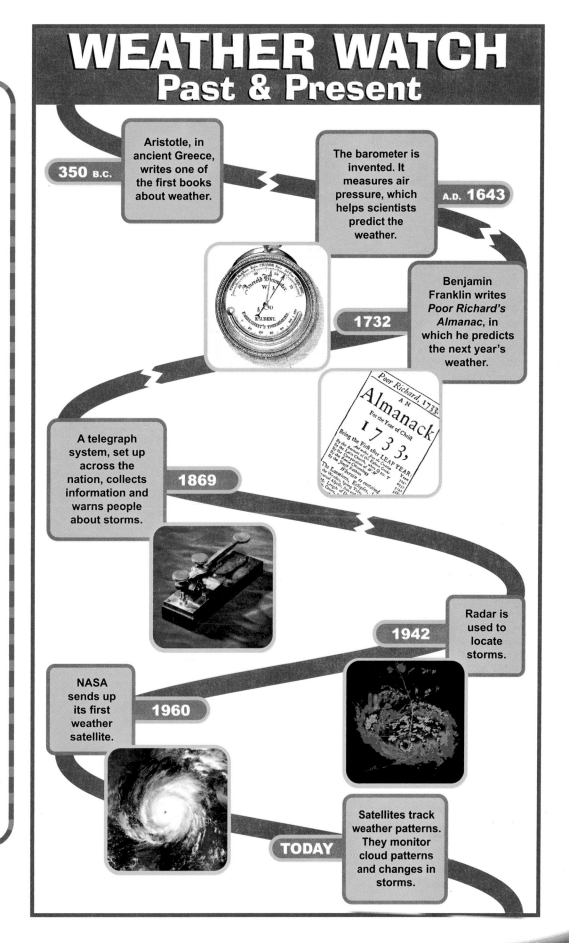

350 B.C. Aristotle, in ancient Greece, writes one of the first books about weather.

The barometer is invented. It measures air pressure, which helps scientists predict the weather. **A.D. 1643**

1732 Benjamin Franklin writes *Poor Richard's Almanac*, in which he predicts the next year's weather.

A telegraph system, set up across the nation, collects information and warns people about storms. **1869**

1942 Radar is used to locate storms.

NASA sends up its first weather satellite. **1960**

TODAY Satellites track weather patterns. They monitor cloud patterns and changes in storms.

On Your Own

Read the article about hurricanes. Then, use the information to finish the time line below about the history of hurricanes. Here's how:

- Write the time line's title and a short introduction.

- Circle the dates in the article. Write them in order on the time line.

- Write a caption for each date.

Hurricane History

A hurricane is a strong storm with high winds. It can cause property damage and harm to people who are in its path. People have studied hurricanes for hundreds of years. Knowing about a hurricane before it reaches an area allows people to prepare and helps them stay safe.

In 1495, Columbus was the first to report a hurricane. He experienced the storm near Hispaniola while on a voyage to the New World.

Ben Franklin was a very curious man. He studied the movement of a hurricane as it traveled up the Atlantic coast in 1743. One hundred years after that, in 1843, the first hurricane warning was posted in the United States.

A century later, in 1943, Joseph Duckworth, a pilot, was the first person to intentionally fly into the eye of a hurricane. Flying into the eye allows pilots to gather information about the strength of the storm.

Hurricanes were first named in 1953. In 1975, the Saffir-Simpson scale was created. This scale makes it possible to estimate how much damage and flooding a hurricane would cause.

Today, satellites and computer models are used to forecast hurricane paths and strengths. This technology allows people to get advance warning of storms.

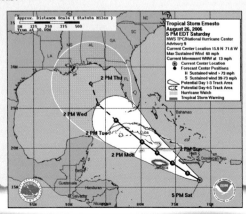

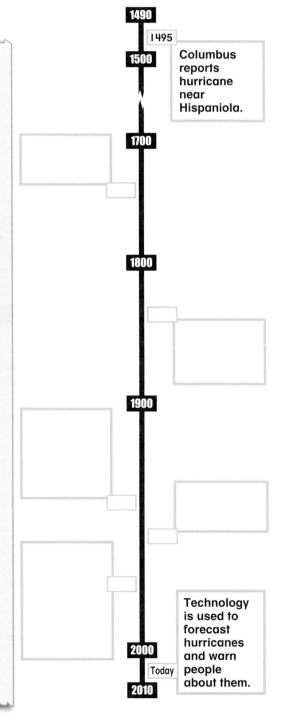

1490

1495 — Columbus reports hurricane near Hispaniola.

1500

1700

1800

1900

2000

Today — Technology is used to forecast hurricanes and warn people about them.

2010

36

Time Lines

A **time line** is a kind of diagram that shows a series of real events and the dates on which they happened. The information is always shown in time order.

Step 1 Read the title to find out the topic or historical period covered in the time line.

Step 2 Find the starting and ending dates for the time line. They tell you how much time is covered.

Step 3 Read the dates in between.

Step 4 Read the labels for each date. They describe each event.

Step 5 Figure out how the events are related.

Practice Your Skills!

1. Put an **X** on the date that shows when the bus boycott began.

2. How long did it take for the bus boycott to succeed? _____

3. Circle the words that tell the name of one of King's famous speeches.

PAIR SHARE Which facts would you choose to show that Martin Luther King, Jr., was an important civil rights leader?

Honoring Martin Luther King, Jr.

A GREAT DAY
Dr. King gives his "I Have a Dream" speech.

In February 1926, educator Dr. Carter G. Woodson began Negro History Week. He chose February because President Abraham Lincoln and abolitionist (AB-uh-LISH-uhn-ist) Frederick Douglass were born in this month. In 1976, during America's bicentennial (bye-sen-TEN-ee-uhl) celebration, the observance was extended to include the entire month. It is during this month, now called "Black History Month," that we remember the **contributions** of civil rights leaders, such as Martin Luther King, Jr.

JANUARY 1929	Martin Luther King, Jr., is born in Atlanta, Georgia, on January 15.
DECEMBER 1955	King leads bus boycott in Montgomery, Alabama, in response to Rosa Parks's arrest.
DECEMBER 1956	Montgomery buses are desegregated.
FEBRUARY 1960	Students in Greensboro, North Carolina, begin lunch-counter sit-in to protest segregation.
AUGUST 1963	King delivers "I Have a Dream" speech in front of more than 150,000 people in Washington, D.C.
APRIL 1968	Martin Luther King, Jr., is assassinated in Memphis, Tennessee, at age 39.

YEARS UNDER SLAVERY

Bridget "Biddy" Mason was born into slavery around 1818. The exact date is not known. She grew up on a Mississippi plantation owned by Robert Smith. Because she was a slave, Biddy Mason was forbidden to learn to read or write.

In 1851, Smith moved his household to California. Mason had to walk behind the wagons, keeping watch to see that the farm animals did not run off.

Bridget "Biddy" Mason

THE ROAD TO FREEDOM

When the group reached California, Smith found out that California did not allow slavery. Smith then tried to move his 14 enslaved workers out of the state. Local African Americans took him to court to prevent this.

Mason was not allowed to speak in court, but she told her story to the judge in private. In 1856, all of Smith's enslaved workers won their freedom.

LIFE IN LOS ANGELES

Biddy Mason settled in Los Angeles where she became a nurse. She helped hundreds of families, rich and poor, black and white.

Ten years after gaining her freedom, Mason bought land just outside of town for $250. She was one of the first African-American women to own land in Los Angeles. As the city of Los Angeles grew, Mason's land became very valuable. She bought more property and became very wealthy.

Mason used her money to help the poor of all races. During the great flood of 1861–1862, Biddy Mason allowed flood victims to use her account at a local grocery store.

BIDDY MASON REMEMBERED

Biddy Mason died in 1891 and was buried in an unmarked grave. However, she was not forgotten. November 16, 1989, was declared Biddy Mason Day. A memorial for her achievements was built in downtown Los Angeles. It is in the park that bears her name.

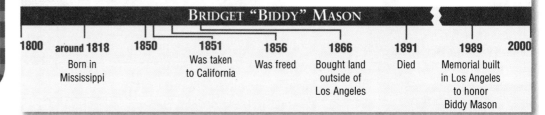

BRIDGET "BIDDY" MASON

1800	around 1818	1850	1851	1856	1866	1891	1989	2000
	Born in Mississippi		Was taken to California	Was freed	Bought land outside of Los Angeles	Died	Memorial built in Los Angeles to honor Biddy Mason	

On Your Own

Below is an article about civil rights leader Fannie Lou Hamer. Use the information in the article to complete a time line of her life. Include important events and the dates when they happened.

Fannie Lou Hamer, an African American, was born on October 16, 1917, in Montgomery County, Mississippi. Her parents farmed land on a plantation. When she was six, she began picking cotton to help her family. She left school at a young age and worked cutting cornstalks to earn money.

Fannie married Perry Hamer in 1944. She and her husband worked on a plantation in Ruleville, Mississippi.

During the 1960s, Fannie became interested in the civil rights movement. She passed the test to become a registered voter, and then she traveled across the South, helping other African Americans register to vote. On June 9, 1963, she and the group with whom she was traveling were arrested for using the "whites only" waiting room at a bus stop. She became even more determined to fight for equal rights.

In 1964, an election year, she spoke about the need to give voting rights to all Americans in front of a committee at the Democratic National Convention. The Voting Rights Act was signed by President Lyndon Johnson in 1965.

Hamer continued to work for better conditions for her people for the rest of her life. She died on March 15, 1977.

Fannie Lou Hamer

1917 _____

____ _____

____ _____

____ _____

____ _____

1977 _____

Sequence

Flying Through

The Wright Brothers' hard work, determination, and inventiveness gave humans the power to reach the sky.

The engine's roar rises in pitch as the plane zooms down the runway, gathering speed and power. Suddenly, the plane tips up and the huge 800,000-pound jet soars into the sky as if it were weightless.

Every day, airplanes like this carry millions of people—and tons of food, medicine, and supplies—across thousands of miles in just a few hours. And it all began about 100 years ago.

THE FLIGHT TO CHANGE THE WORLD
On December 17, 1903, over a wet, windswept field in Kitty Hawk, North Carolina, the Wright Brothers flew the world's first **successful** airplane—the *Flyer*.

Orville Wright was the first to pilot the *Flyer*, which the brothers built by hand. Lying facedown, he steered the plane by shifting his hips and hands. That first flight lasted only 12 seconds and covered just 120 feet—less than the wingspan of some of today's commercial (kuh-MER-shuhl) planes. Yet it was an amazing victory, marking the first time humans reached the sky in a flying machine that was heavier than air.

News of the brothers' success soon spread, inspiring

Follow along with the time line to see achievements in aviation over the past 100 years.

Orville and Wilbur Wright make the world's first successful airplane flight.

The Bell X-1 *Glamorous Glennis* breaks the sound barrier for the first time (approximately 670 mph). Charles Yeager is the pilot.

1903   **1927**   **1932**   **194**

Charles Lindbergh makes the first solo nonstop flight across the Atlantic on the *Spirit of St. Louis*.

Amelia Earhart is the first woman to fly solo across the Atlantic.

HISTORY

INTO THE WIND
Airplane adventurers take off with a running start to fly a copy of a Wright Brothers' plane.

inventors and adventurers to new achievements in flight. The first century of **aviation**, the science of building and flying planes, had begun.

After their first flight, the Wright Brothers realized that they still had a lot of work to do on their invention. While the 1903 *Flyer* did fly, it was underpowered and difficult to control. For two years, the Wrights made many flights, fine-tuning the controls, engine, and design of their airplane. At first, they could only fly in a straight line for less than a minute. But by the end of 1905, they were flying figure eights and staying in the air for more than a half hour.

LIFE AFTER THE WRIGHTS

Powered flight forever changed the way people travel and do business. Airplanes transformed how wars are fought and paved the way for space flight. Police forces use planes to search for missing people. Helicopters rescue the sick by taking them to hospitals that are often unreachable by car.

The Wright Brothers' invention made the world more connected. We have since traveled to the moon and space shuttles orbit our planet. All of these amazing advances can be traced back to that windy day at Kitty Hawk.

Soviet cosmonaut Yuri Gagarin is the first person to go to space. U.S. astronaut Alan Shepard follows one month later.

Columbia, the first reusable space shuttle to orbit Earth, launches. The shuttle has since returned to space over 100 times.

The U.S. military launches sleek, tailless robot planes—the first unpiloted planes developed to carry weapons into combat.

1961   1969   1981 1988   2002

The first humans land and walk on the moon.

The U.S. military unveils the B-2 *Stealth Bomber*, undetectable by radar.

Sequence

Reread "Flying Through History." Fill in the graphic organizer with what you think are the six most important accomplishments in the history of flight. Put the dates and the events that you choose in time order.

LANDMARKS IN FLIGHT

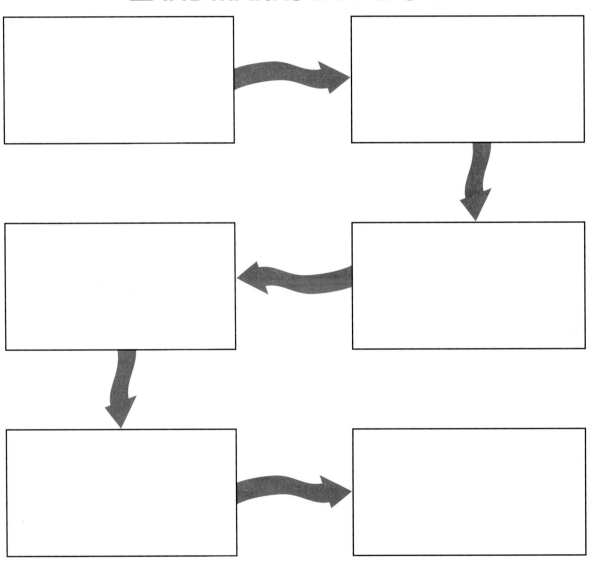

 Use the organizer above to retell your choices for the six top achievements in the history of flight. Include as many details as you can remember for each event.

Writing Frame

Use the information in your graphic organizer to fill in the sequence of events in the writing frame.

The first event in the history of flight was in 1903, when _____

_____

_____.

After that, in _____, _____

_____.

Next, _____ in _____

_____.

Then, in _____, _____.

After that, in _____, _____

_____.

Finally, _____

_____ in _____.

 Use the writing frame above as a model to describe another sequence of events in the history of science. You may want to write about the exploration of Mars or the life of a famous scientist. Look in your science textbook if you need facts to help you fill in the frame.

Graphs

Have you ever heard the expression "A picture is worth a thousand words"? That is really true about a graph. A **graph** is a picture that shows information about amounts, or numbers. A graph tells you a lot with very few words. It lets you compare and contrast quickly and easily.

One kind of graph is a **bar graph**. A bar graph uses bars to compare amounts. The graph on this page is a **pictograph**, or picture graph. Each picture stands for an amount. The **key** tells you the amount each picture stands for. Here's how to read a pictograph.

Step 1 **Read the title and the introduction to find out what information the graph shows.** This graph will be about how much water is used for washing different things.

Step 2 **Read the labels for each row.** This graph is horizontal. The labels are on the left side of the graph. They tell you some activities that use water. Other graphs may be vertical, with the labels at the bottom.

Step 3 **Look at the key to find out the amount each symbol stands for.** Next to each label, there is a row of pictures. The key shows that each drop of water stands for about 2 gallons.

Step 4 **Read the graph.** Read the first label. Then figure out the total number of gallons of water used for that activity. Since each drop equals about 2 gallons, you can count the number of drops and multiply by 2. Or you can count the drops by 2's.

Step 5 **Compare and contrast the information on the graph.** For example, what activity uses the most water? How much water does it use? Which uses the least water? How much water does that use?

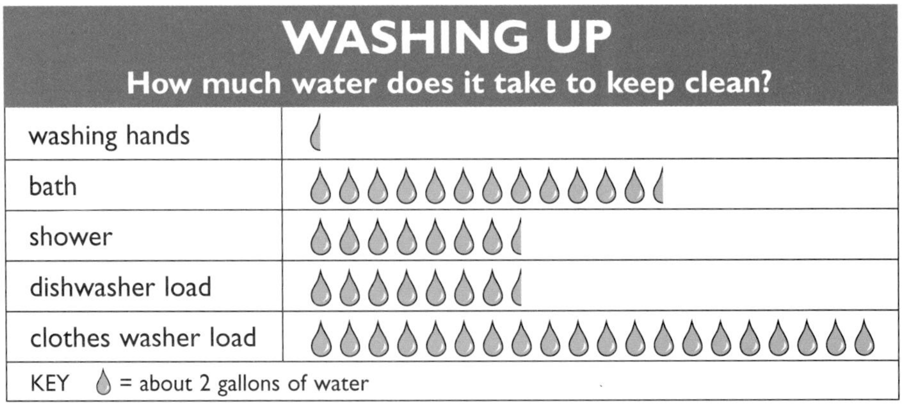

Practice Your Skills!

1. Put an **X** on the activity that uses the most water.

2. Circle the two activities that use about the same amount of water.

3 How much water is used for a shower? for a bath?

PAIR SHARE How could people cut down on the use of water for washing?

WASHING UP How much water does it take to keep clean?	
washing hands	⬦
bath	⬦⬦⬦⬦⬦⬦⬦⬦⬦⬦⬦⬦
shower	⬦⬦⬦⬦⬦⬦⬦⬦⬦
dishwasher load	⬦⬦⬦⬦⬦⬦⬦
clothes washer load	⬦⬦⬦⬦⬦⬦⬦⬦⬦⬦⬦⬦⬦⬦⬦⬦⬦
KEY ⬦ = about 2 gallons of water	

A HANDY WAY TO STAY HEALTHY

If you don't think washing your hands is important, you should meet Lacie Boothe.

Last winter, after a long day of handling cattle, sheep, and horses on her family's farm in Pulaski, Virginia, Lacie felt sick. In the middle of the night, Lacie's grandmother rushed her to the hospital.

"My stomach felt like it was turning inside out," says Lacie, 9. "The doctors said I was sick because I had picked up **germs** on my hands. I hadn't washed my hands, so I swallowed the germs."

Unfriendly germs don't just hang around farms.

Kids can pick up germs at home just by flushing the toilet or playing outside in the backyard.

Lacie

HIDDEN ENEMIES

Billions of tiny organisms, or microscopic animals, live on almost every inch of our bodies, including our mouths, armpits, and hands. Most of these invisible creatures, known as **bacteria** (bak-TIR-ee-uh), live on our skin, feasting on dead skin cells.

Some of these organisms actually help us by producing vitamins and helping us to digest (dye-JEST) food.

But other bacteria can invade our bodies, spreading illness and **disease.** These germs linger in the air, water, soil, and on everything we touch— from pencils and backpacks to soccer balls and computers.

INTO THE BODY

While some harmful bacteria storm our bodies through our noses and eyes, most often they enter our systems through our mouths.

"If you are playing with a soccer ball covered in dirt and bite your nails or stick your fingers in your mouth, you may be swallowing hundreds, even thousands of bacteria, some of which can make you sick," says Ralph Cordell, a scientist at the Centers for Disease Control in Atlanta, Georgia. So, wash up to stay healthy!

GERM HANGOUTS

Bacteria are tiny germs that live on almost all surfaces. The graph shows some common surfaces and the number of germs per square inch that live on them.

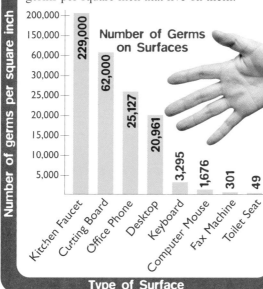

Number of Germs on Surfaces

Number of germs per square inch (y-axis): 200,000 / 150,000 / 60,000 / 30,000 / 25,000 / 20,000 / 15,000 / 10,000 / 5,000

- Kitchen Faucet: 229,000
- Cutting Board: 62,000
- Office Phone: 25,127
- Desktop: 20,961
- Keyboard: 3,295
- Computer Mouse: 1,676
- Fax Machine: 301
- Toilet Seat: 49

Type of Surface

45

On Your Own

Below is an article about water use. Read the article and the bar graph. Think about how the information in this bar graph adds to what you already know about water and keeping clean. Remember to:

- Read the graph's title.
- Read the labels.
- Read the symbols or numbers.

We Need Water

All living things need water. Humans use water for drinking, for washing themselves, for keeping items in their homes clean, for watering lawns, and for recreation.

There is a limited amount of fresh water on Earth. We need to use it wisely. We can conserve water by changing the way we do certain things each day. These changes may seem to save small amounts, but if everyone saves water we can conserve this important resource.

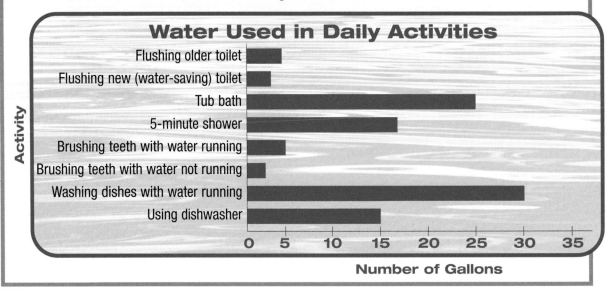

Water Used in Daily Activities

Activity:
- Flushing older toilet
- Flushing new (water-saving) toilet
- Tub bath
- 5-minute shower
- Brushing teeth with water running
- Brushing teeth with water not running
- Washing dishes with water running
- Using dishwasher

Number of Gallons: 0 5 10 15 20 25 30 35

Write three questions about the graph. When you're done, change papers with a partner. Answer each other's questions.

1._____

2._____

3._____

Graphs

Many social studies books and articles contain graphs to go with the text. A **graph** is a kind of picture that shows amounts, or numbers, at a glance. A graph can show the same information that is in the text, but it helps you "picture" the information and makes it easier to understand and quicker to read.

A **circle graph**, also called a pie graph, is divided into "slices," or sections. It shows how the parts fit into the whole.

Step 1 **Read the title to find out what the graph is about.**
The circle graph below shows the population of Washington, D.C.

Step 2 **Look at the sections.** This graph has seven sections, or "slices." Each section shows one group of people. You can see how each section compares to the whole—how each group compares to the total population.

Step 3 **Use the labels to find out what is being compared.**
The labels on the graph below name the groups of people who live in Washington, D.C. A line connects the label to the correct section of the graph.

Step 4 **Compare and contrast the information shown on the graph.** For example, think about which group of people make up more than half the population of Washington, D.C. Which is the second largest group?

Practice Your Skills!

1. Circle the label that tells which group has the largest number of people in Washington, D.C.

2. Put an **X** on the number that tells how many Asians live in Washington, D.C.

3. Underline the word in the article that means "varied" or "different."

PAIR SHARE How would you compare the populations of African Americans, Asians, and Caucasians in Washington, D.C.?

A People Place

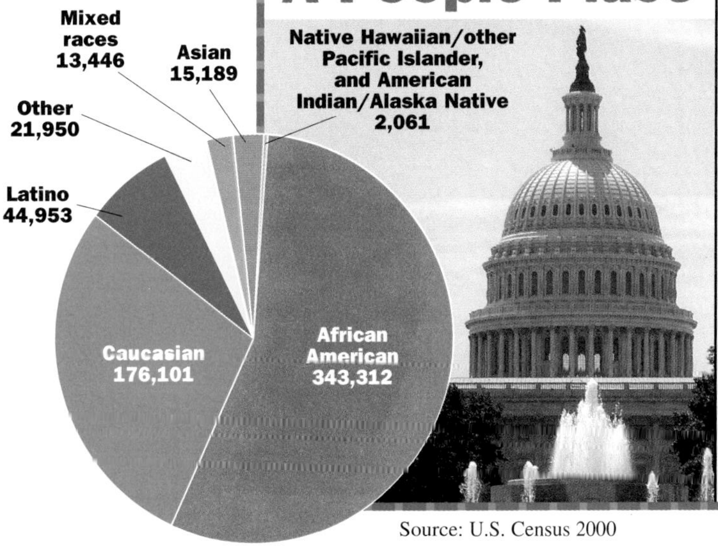

Mixed races 13,446
Asian 15,189
Native Hawaiian/other Pacific Islander, and American Indian/Alaska Native 2,061
Other 21,950
Latino 44,953
Caucasian 176,101
African American 343,312

Washington, D.C., is home to lots of famous buildings, including the White House, the Capitol, and the National Air and Space Museum. It's also home to thousands of everyday people who live, work, and play there. Like most cities, Washington, D.C., has a **diverse** mix of many people and neighborhoods.

Source: U.S. Census 2000

The Population of Washington, D.C.

Before You Read

Preview the article. Check (✔) the special features it has.

_____ introduction
_____ headings
_____ graph
_____ pronunciations
_____ labels
_____ boldfaced words

As You Read

• Did you read the graph title to find out the topic?
❏ Yes ❏ No

• Did you study each section?
❏ Yes ❏ No

• Did you read the labels? ❏ Yes ❏ No

• Explain how you read the graph.

After You Read

1. When did Asian immigrants enter the United States?

2. Where were the largest group of immigrants in California in 2000 from?

PAIR SHARE How do we know about what happened at Angel Island?

COMING TO AMERICA

At the same time immigrants from Europe were crossing the Atlantic, almost a million Asian immigrants were making the three-week trip across the Pacific Ocean.

ANGEL ISLAND

From 1910 to 1940, Asian **immigrants** entered the United States by way of Angel Island, located in San Francisco Bay. Angel Island was sometimes called "the Ellis Island of the West Coast," but immigrants there had a far more difficult time than the Europeans entering at Ellis Island.

Officials at Angel Island were not welcoming to the Asians. They set up many **obstacles** for Asian immigrants trying to enter. Immigrants faced extreme crowding, endless questioning, and days and days of waiting at the Angel Island Immigration Station. Those who were **detained** the longest were the Chinese, who often waited for weeks and even months.

A PLACE TO WAIT

About 175,000 Chinese passed through Angel Island. Their first sight of a pleasant hillside with palm trees gave them no clue as to what awaited them. The buildings in which the immigrants were detained were wooden **barracks** surrounded by guard towers and barbed-wire fences with locked gates.

Immigrants were separated by nationality and gender into crowded rooms. Husbands and wives were not allowed to see each other until both had been cleared to enter the country. Feeling like prisoners, many of the Chinese detainees expressed their sadness, anger, and pain by writing poems, which they carved on the wooden walls.

> There are tens of thousands of poems composed on these walls.
> They are all cries of complaint and sadness.
> The day I am rid of this prison and attain success,
> I must remember that this chapter once existed.
> —By One From Xiangshan (Poem 31)

PRESERVING HISTORY

A raging fire at Angel Island caused the station to be moved to San Francisco in 1941. The island became a California State Park in 1962. Since then, people have worked to restore the buildings. The wooden barracks, with their firsthand accounts carved on the walls, have already been opened for visitors.

About 75 percent of the Chinese and Japanese in California have their roots in Angel Island. They and many others hope that Angel Island will eventually be made a national **landmark** to be remembered by all of us.

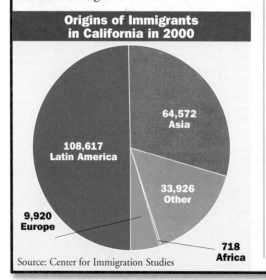

Origins of Immigrants in California in 2000

- 64,572 Asia
- 108,617 Latin America
- 33,926 Other
- 9,920 Europe
- 718 Africa

Source: Center for Immigration Studies

On Your Own

Read the article below about immigration to the United States in 2002. Then complete the circle graph to show the information discussed in the text.

- Underline the sentence that tells about the largest number of immigrants. Circle the name of the continent and the percentage.

- Find the largest section of the graph.

- Label the section. Write the continent and the percentage next to the line.

- Do the same thing for the second-largest percentage.

- Continue in this way until you finish labeling all the sections of the graph.

Immigrants Come From Many Continents

In 2002, a total of 1,063,732 immigrants were admitted to the United States. They came from each of the continents, except Antarctica.

The largest number, approximately 40 percent, came from North America. Immigrants from Asia made up about 32 percent of people admitted to the U.S. Immigrants from Europe made up almost 16 percent. People from South America totaled roughly 7 percent, and immigrants from Africa made up slightly more than 5 percent of the total. The smallest percentage, about 0.5 percent, came from Australia/Oceania.

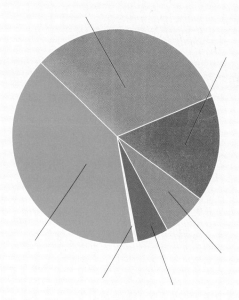

Immigrants Admitted to the United States by Continent, 2002

Source: *2002 Yearbook of Immigration Statistics*, U.S. Citizenship and Immigration Services.

Compare/Contrast

Before You Read

Vocabulary Put a check in the column that shows what the connection is between each boldfaced word and the other word(s).

What's the Connection?

Words	Synonyms	Examples
canals tubes		
system nervous system muscular system		
organs body parts		
maneuver move		
vessels arteries		

As You Read

Text Structure This article compares and contrasts the way body systems function on Earth and in space. To keep track of the comparisons, underline the words that tell what happens on Earth. Circle the words that tell what happens in space.

Text Feature How does the graph help you understand the article?

After You Read

1. Why might you have motion sickness during the first few days in space?

2. Study the graph. On which two planets would you weigh the most?

3. Choose a body system. Compare and contrast how it functions on Earth with the way it functions in space.

Could your body go to Mars?

Space travel might change you in surprising ways. Body systems work to keep humans alive. Scientists at NASA are studying what would happen to the human body during a long space trip. Read on, then decide: Would you like to go to Mars?

No Fun at Lunch

Fluid-filled canals in your inner ear help your brain know right side up from upside down. But leave Earth's atmosphere, and you leave the planet's gravity pull behind. Without its strong pull, your balancing organs will have no sense of up or down. Your **sensory system**—which relays information about your body to your brain—won't be able to do its job. For the first few days, you'll have the universe's worst case of motion sickness.

Brittle Bones

Your bones make up your **skeletal system**—the frame that holds your body together. On Earth, the pressure of your body weight causes your bones to grow thick and strong. Without this pressure, bones become fragile. In NASA studies, astronauts lost up to 1/50th of their bone mass every month they were in space.

The Skinny in Space

In the zero gravity of space, objects—including your body—are nearly weightless. So your **muscular system**, or the muscles in your body, doesn't get much of a workout. Unused muscles **atrophy** (A-truh-fee), or shrink. After weeks in space, thigh muscles look like a peeled apple left out to dry.

Your Weight in Space

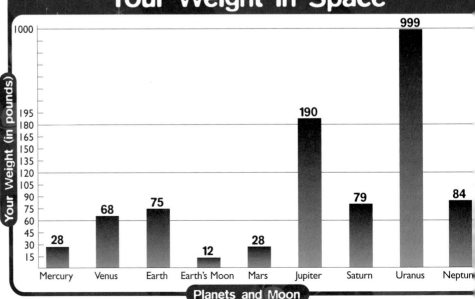

Your Weight (in pounds)

Planets and Moon	Weight
Mercury	28
Venus	68
Earth	75
Earth's Moon	12
Mars	28
Jupiter	190
Saturn	79
Uranus	999
Neptune	84

Weak Beater

Your heart, too, will shrink in space. As the heart muscle weakens, it pumps less oxygen-rich blood through the vessels in your circulatory system. With less oxygen reaching the brain and other organs, astronauts feel tired. They rest more. They use their heart even less. By the end of six months, every beat of an astronaut's heart could be pumping just a little more than half of the blood it did on Earth.

What a Nerve!

On a journey to Mars there's no stopping for breaks. There won't be much for astronauts to do during the long, dull flight. Without stimulation, their **nervous system**—the body's chief control system—will weaken. Their reaction times and hand-eye coordination will be slower. They would lose at Nintendo and Snap. They might not be able to maneuver the ship safely onto Mars's surface.

Quick Fix-Up

With exercise, your body can fight some of these changes. For instance, special treadmills and a weight machine allowed cosmonauts on the way to Mir space station to maintain strong muscles. But even with fancy equipment, the journey to Mars will be difficult. It's our solar system's toughest road trip so far.

Planet Superlatives

Largest, most massive planet	JUPITER
Fastest orbiting planet	MERCURY
Most moons	JUPITER (39)
Hottest planet	VENUS
Greatest amount of liquid, surface water	EARTH

Compare/Contrast

Reread "Could Your Body Go to Mars?" Fill in the graphic organizer with details that compare and contrast how body systems function on Earth and in space.

On Earth   **In Space**

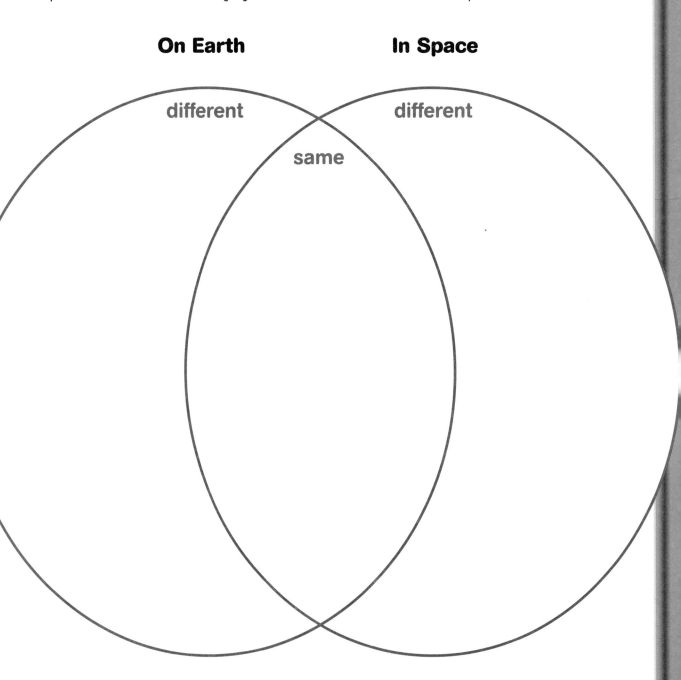

different   different

same

Use the graphic organizer above to retell "Could Your Body Go to Mars?" in your own words. Include as much information as you can remember.

Writing Frame

Use the information in your graphic organizer to fill in the writing frame.

The ways in which body systems work on Earth and in space are similar in

some ways. They are similar because _____

_____.

However, in many ways body systems work differently on Earth and in

space. For example, on Earth, your sensory system _____

_____. But in space, _____

_____.

On Earth, your bones _____.

However, in space, bones _____.

On Earth, muscles _____. But, in space, _____

_____.

On Earth, your heart pumps oxygen-rich blood through your blood vessels.

However, in space the heart _____ so it pumps less blood.

 Use the writing frame above as a model to compare and contrast how simple machines, such as pulleys, levers, and wheels work. Look in your science textbook if you need facts that will help you fill in the frame.

Diagrams

Nonfiction often contains diagrams to go with the text. A **diagram** is a labeled drawing that shows how something works or how the parts of something are arranged. For example, a diagram can show the bones in the body or the life cycle of a plant. The diagram helps you "picture" the information and makes it easier to understand. Here's how to read a diagram.

Step 1 **Read the title to find out what the diagram shows.** The diagram below shows how a drought forms.

Step 2 **Read the introduction to learn the main idea about the topic.** The introduction tells us that a drought, a period of unusually dry weather, causes a risk of wildfire.

Step 3 **Read the labels. They name parts of the diagram.** Each label details either a part of the process of how rain forms during a normal water cycle or the weather patterns that cause a drought. Follow the line from each label to the diagram.

Practice Your Skills!

1. Put an **X** on what happens first during a normal water cycle.

2. Circle the last thing that happens during a normal water cycle.

PAIR SHARE Discuss the major differences between a normal water cycle and a drought. How are plants and animals affected by a drought?

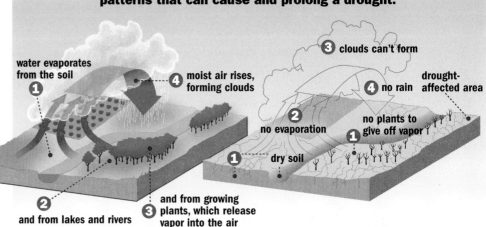

THIRSTY LAND

Wildfires burn in the West every year. Most experts agree that a drought, or a period of unusually dry weather, is largely to blame.

How a Drought Forms

The diagram on the left shows how rain forms during a normal water cycle. The one on the right shows patterns that can cause and prolong a drought.

water evaporates from the soil
①
④ moist air rises, forming clouds
③ clouds can't form
④ no rain
drought-affected area
② no evaporation
① no plants to give off vapor
① dry soil
② and from lakes and rivers
③ and from growing plants, which release vapor into the air

NORMAL WATER CYCLE   **DROUGHT**

FORESTS ON FIRE

Forest fires can be caused by weather conditions or by the carelessness of people.

California Forest Fires

Mojave Desert
Wind
Santa Monica Mountains
Los Angeles
Wind
Pacific Ocean

Winds blow over the dry Mojave Desert and travel toward the Pacific Ocean.

There are some places where you can expect wildfires. In California, fires burn 50,000 to 500,000 acres of land every year. Some of the plants that live there have oily sap. They can survive the dry, hot summers, but if they catch fire they explode into flame. Grasses grow thick during the spring rains and then die. They dry into a thick layer of straw that burns fast, making a very hot fire.

Fires can start wherever there's fuel to burn. California has plenty of fuel and a hot, dry wind that blows every year between mid-September and late October. This wind, called the Santa Ana, passes over the inland desert, losing moisture and gaining heat, and rushes toward the ocean to the West. It fans the flames and makes fighting the fires nearly impossible.

Forests are a natural storehouse of fuel for a fire. During a dry summer, dead trees and low brush in a forest can burst into flame wherever

lightning strikes. Rain usually puts these fires out. But sometimes the combination of dry fuel, hot dry air, and strong winds is just right for a major forest fire.

In 1988, Yellowstone National Park was burned by several such fires at once. Lightning struck in two places. A worker dropped a lit cigarette in another place. On the worst day of the fire, more than 600 square kilometers (about 230 square miles) of forest burned. Clouds of smoke that looked like storm clouds rose into the atmosphere. Smoke blocked the sun and drifted far beyond the park.

Firefighters work hard to control fires like those in Yellowstone and California, many of which are caused by people. But long before humans learned how to start or put out a fire, prairies and forests burned every year. Both kinds of land recovered, as they have in Yellowstone and in California.

On Your Own

These diagrams show cross sections of the bark of a Jeffrey pine tree. As you study the diagrams and read the text, ask yourself, "What is special about the bark that helps the tree survive forest fires that don't get too hot?"

Jeffrey Pine Bark

Jeffrey pine trees live in the warmest and driest places in the Lake Tahoe basin, an area where there are many forest fires. The tree's bark smells like vanilla!

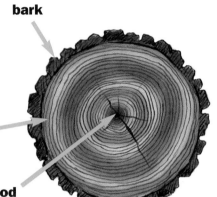

bark

cambium

heartwood

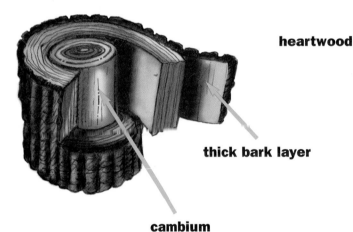

thick bark layer

cambium

The bark of a mature Jeffrey pine makes it possible for the tree to survive forest fires that do not get too hot. Young Jeffrey pine trees cannot survive a fire's heat.

Write three questions about the diagrams and text. When you're done, change papers with a partner. Answer each other's questions.

1. _____

2. _____

3. _____

4. On another sheet of paper, draw a diagram of a tree near your home or school.

Diagrams

A **diagram** is a labeled picture that shows the parts of something or a process. Here's how to read a diagram.

Step 1 **Read the title to find out what the diagram shows.** The diagram below shows the inside of an Iroquois longhouse.

Step 2 **Read the introduction to learn the main idea about the topic.** The introduction tells us that this article is about the Iroquois Nation and the homes they lived in long ago.

Step 3 **Read the labels. They name parts of the diagram.** Each label details something that could be found in the longhouse. Follow the line from each label to the diagram.

Step 4 **Be sure to read the caption.** This caption gives additional information about the Iroquois longhouse.

Practice Your Skills!

1. Circle the label that names the place where people slept.

2. Add a label on the dotted line.

3. Underline the phrase that means "a place to keep things."

PAIR SHARE What were the advantages and disadvantages of living in a longhouse with several other families?

Iroquois Longhouse

The Iroquois lived long ago in what is now New York State along the St. Lawrence River. Their home was called a longhouse.

Iroquois longhouses were longer than they were wide. They had door openings at both ends. During the winter, these openings were covered with skins. There were no windows on the longhouse walls.

The walls of the longhouse were made from elm bark that was cut into rectangular slabs to be used for roof shingles and wall siding. A smoke hole in the roof allowed smoke from the fire to escape.

Labels: smoke hole, bark strips (instead of nails), storage area, bunk bed, post, sheets of bark, pole, drying corn, one of two doors, storage area, post, fire area

These homes from the 1600s housed several families.

THE END OF THE TRAIL

By 1860, thousands of pioneers had traveled along the Oregon Trail in search of new homes. At the end of the trail, they found what they had dreamed of—land that they could farm. They began the hard work of building new lives for themselves.

Building a Home

Since there were no homes or businesses nearby, the **pioneers** had to provide for themselves. First, they **cleared** their plot of land. The trees that were cut down were used to build a log cabin. The roof was shingles (SHING-gulz) made from bark. The floor was made of split logs.

Inside the Cabin

Most of the early homes had only one room. The same room was used as a kitchen, workroom, family room, and bedroom. A family might have a table and chairs, a cupboard (KUH-berd) for dishes, and benches made of split logs. Clothes were kept in chests or trunks. The family slept on wooden beds with straw mattresses, covered with handmade quilts. For the baby, there was a cradle.

Shelves along the walls held food supplies, such as flour and sugar. Pots and pans hung from wooden pegs in the wall.

A stone fireplace heated the cabin, cooked the food, and provided light. A butter churn, spinning wheel, candle mold, and other tools allowed the family to make the things they needed. Days were spent doing the many **chores** that it took just to survive.

butter churn
fireplace
spinning wheel
table
cupboard
bed
farm tools

On Your Own

Read the article below. Then use the information to complete the diagram of the sod house. Draw a line from each label to the correct part of the diagram. Provide a title and caption for the diagram.

Sod Homes

Until pioneers could build permanent homes, they built homes made of sod. Lumber was expensive to buy and not readily available. But the prairie did provide a large resource that the settlers could use—sod.

Sod houses began to dot the landscape. The sod squares, cut from the soil, had long grass roots in them that were tough yet flexible. Not only were the walls constructed of sod, but most roofs were covered in sod, as well. Only a small amount of lumber was used for a door, the roof frame, and one or more windows. These houses were cool in the summer and warm in the winter. But, as soon as a farm family could afford it, they bought lumber to build a pioneer cabin.

Title _____

Labels

sod roof covering

chimney

wooden roof frame

wooden door frame

window

sod blocks

_____

Caption _____

_____

Text Structure

Problem/Solution

Help for

Gray wolves are reclaiming the thick forests, mountains,

Before You Read

Vocabulary Use the words to complete the sentences.

pack   fitted
rare   monitor

What's the Word?

1. It is _____ to see gray wolves in the western part of the United States.

2. Scientists _____ animal populations to learn about the animal's habits.

3. In order to keep track of where wolves roam, the animals are _____ with special collars.

4. Lions hunt alone, but wolves hunt in a _____.

As You Read

Text Structure This article tells how gray wolves are being reintroduced in the West. The article contains information about the **problem** that caused this to be necessary and the **solution** that has been tried. To keep track of the problem and solution, underline phrases that describe the problem. Circle phrases that describe the solution.

Text Feature How does the diagram help you understand the article?

After You Read

1. Why is it important to restore a balance in nature?

2. Study the diagram. Explain how the food chain works.

3. Do you think the gray wolf should be reintroduced in the West? Why or why not?

HOW THEY HOWL! Scientists believe wolves howl to mark their territory. A grown wolf howls at the moon (left) and a pup practices his howl (inset).

A howl rises in the frosty sky. Is it a warning? An announcement? A call to a family member?

In some places around the country, it could be a pack of gray wolves, announcing, "We're back!"

Gray wolves once **roamed** freely over most of the United States. But then there was a problem. Over the years, settlers drove them out. By the last century, wolves had almost disappeared from the United States. Thanks to recent efforts to protect wolves and bring them back to the wilderness, gray wolves are roaming once again in several areas of the United States.

Wolves are fascinating animals. Though many people are thrilled about their return, others fear wolf attacks on humans, pets, and farm animals.

BRINGING BACK THE PACK

"Wolves are rare, precious animals," says Ed Banks of the U.S. Fish and Wildlife Service.

Banks coordinates programs that try to solve the problem of wolves becoming **extinct**. He and his team have **reintroduced**, or brought back, gray wolves in the West. In 1995, Banks and his team caught several wolves in Canada. The team brought the wolves by helicopter to the United States, and fitted them with radio collars to keep track of them. The team then set the wolves free in **wilderness** areas of Montana, Idaho, and Wyoming (wye-OH-ming).

Howlers

and plains in parts of the United States.

Before reintroduction, wolves had disappeared from these areas. Now, over 800 wolves live there. Arizona and New Mexico also have a gray wolf success story.

"Our goal is to save the **species** (SPEE-sheez)," says Victoria Fox, who works with teams that bring Mexican gray wolves from zoos and refuges, in order to turn them loose. Mexican gray wolves are just one of 32 gray wolf species.

Before the reintroduction program started in New Mexico and Arizona in 1998, the Mexican gray wolf was extinct in the wild. Today, about 21 Mexican gray wolves roam the area's pine woods and an unknown number of wild pups have been born.

BALANCING ACT

Many people believe that wolves can help restore a balance in nature. For example, when wolves kill an animal such as a deer, they leave some of its body behind. This provides food for coyotes, eagles, lynx, bears, and other scavengers, or animals that eat dead animals or garbage.

Yet many people who live near the wolves' **territory** feel that the animals are a threat. Every year, wolves kill dozens of sheep, cows, and other farm animals. They may also, on occasion, attack people and their pets.

Can people and wolves live side by side in peace? It's up to humans. Wildlife organizations monitor wolves closely. They often repay ranchers for livestock killed by wolves. With cooperation, many people hope that wolves and humans can share the land.

WOLF FUN FACTS

Wolf pack members lick the leader's nose to show respect.

* Wolves live in packs, or family groups. The strongest wolf is the pack leader.

* There are 32 types of gray wolves, including eastern timber wolves, Labrador wolves, arctic wolves, and tundra wolves.

* Although they're called gray wolves, the fur can be black, brown, gray, white, or a mixture of colors.

* Wolves and dogs are distantly related. Many scientists believe that wolves are ancestors of dogs.

* Wolves are carnivores, or meat-eaters. Pups eat meat that adult wolves have swallowed, digested, and thrown up for them. Yuck!

How the Food Chain Balances Nature

Animals depend on plants and other animals for food. This feeding relationship is called a food chain. This diagram shows how a food chain works.

PRODUCERS	→	HERBIVORES	→	CARNIVORES
Plants and other organisms that provide food for animals make up the first link in the food chain.		These are animals that eat only plants. Called prey, they are hunted by meat eaters.		These meat eaters feed on herbivores. They are also called predators. When they die, their remains fertilize the ground and help plants grow.

Problem/Solution

Reread "Help for Howlers." Fill in the graphic organizer to show the main problem discussed in the text, the attempted solutions, and the end result.

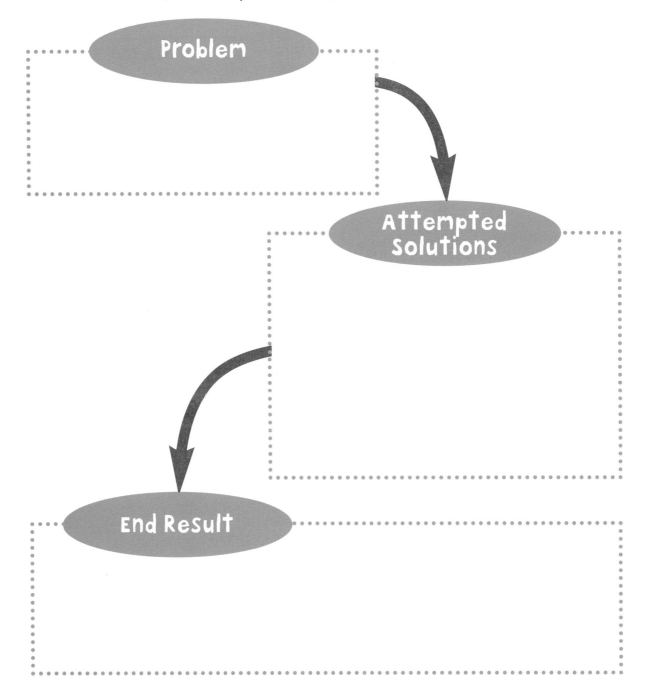

Problem

Attempted Solutions

End Result

Retell

Use the graphic organizer above to retell "Help for Howlers" in your own words. Include as much information as you can remember.

Writing Frame

Use the information in your graphic organizer to fill in the writing frame.

Gray wolves once roamed freely in the western United States,

but not anymore.

The problem was that _____

_____

_____.

The problem happened because _____

_____.

The problem was finally solved when _____

_____

_____.

Now gray wolves are making a comeback.

 Use the writing frame above as a model to write a paragraph about another animal in danger, why the problem happened, and what people have done to try to solve the problem. Look in your science textbook if you need facts that will help you fill in the frame.

LESSON 19

Text Feature

Headings

Most textbook articles present information in a way that alerts you to the main ideas in the text. Writers of these books and magazines want their readers to "get it." So, they put in clues, such as the title, an introduction, and headings, to help the reader.

Step 1 **Read the title to find out what the article is about.** The article below is about a growing population.

Step 2 **Read the introduction to learn the main idea of the article.** The introduction explains that Hispanics are the largest and fastest-growing ethnic group in the U.S. This is the main idea of the article.

Step 3 **Read the headings to find out the main idea of each section.** Headings get you ready for what you are going to read.

Step 4 **Look for details to get additional facts.** Under each heading are details about the main idea. One detail is that Hispanics are almost 13 percent of the U.S. population.

Practice Your Skills!

1. Circle the title.

2. Underline the headings of this article.

3. What is the purpose of the introduction?

PAIR SHARE What is one important detail under each heading?

37 Million—and Growing

Hispanic Americans are now the largest American minority and the fastest-growing ethnic group.

KID POWER! Over 8.8 million Latino kids live in the United States.

Hispanics: Who They Are

Today, 37 million Hispanics, or Latinos, live in the United States—up from 35.3 million in 2000. Hispanics are almost 13 percent of the U.S. population. That means that roughly one in eight Americans claims Hispanic **heritage** (HER-uh-tij). Hispanics, or Latinos, are people who were born in or have **ancestors** from Spain, Mexico, or Spanish-speaking countries in South and Central America.

Census Report

The news comes from the latest report from the U.S. Census Bureau. The Bureau conducts a **census**, or an official count of the people living in the United States, every 10 years. The last census was in 2000. Since then, the Hispanic population has grown by 4.1 percent, or 12 million people.

"Anybody that travels around can see Latinos everywhere, trying to reach the American dream," says Hector Flores, president of the League of United Latin American Citizens.

Practice Your Skills!

Before You Read

Preview the article. Check (✔) the special features it has.

____ title
____ pronunciations
____ headings
____ graph
____ introduction
____ captions
____ photos
____ boldfaced words

As You Read

- Did you read the title of the article to learn the topic?
  ❏ Yes ❏ No

- Did you read the headings?
  ❏ Yes ❏ No

- Did you look for details under each heading?
  ❏ Yes ❏ No

- Explain how you read the article.

After You Read

1. What is the main idea of this article?

2. What information did you learn from the headings?

PAIR SHARE Which details would you choose to show that Hispanic Americans have made important contributions in their chosen fields?

CELEBRATE HISPANIC HERITAGE!

Many Hispanic Americans have made important contributions in their chosen fields.

ROBERTO CLEMENTE
MAJOR LEAGUE BASEBALL PLAYER

Roberto Clemente was born in 1934. A Puerto Rican, he drew attention to the excellence of Latin American players in the Major Leagues. A great fielder and hitter, he was the first Puerto Rican to be voted Most Valuable Player. Clemente was killed in a plane crash on the way to take supplies to earthquake victims in Nicaragua on New Year's Eve, 1972.

ANTONIA C. NOVELLO
DOCTOR AND FORMER UNITED STATES SURGEON GENERAL

Antonia Novello is Puerto Rican. She was born in 1944. In 1990, she became the first Hispanic person—and the first woman as well—to be appointed as surgeon general, the chief doctor in the United States. As a child, she had a **chronic** illness that hurt her digestion, causing her great suffering. She never forgot that experience. As surgeon (SER-gen) general, Novello campaigned (kam-PANED) especially for better care for children.

GLORIA ESTEFAN
SINGER AND MUSICIAN

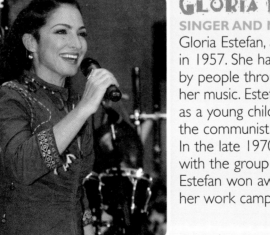

Gloria Estefan, a Cuban American, was born in 1957. She has been loved and admired by people throughout the world for her music. Estefan came to Miami, Florida, as a young child when her parents fled the communist government of Fidel Castro. In the late 1970s, she became a singer with the group Miami Sound Machine. Estefan won awards for her music and for her work campaigning against drugs.

On Your Own

Below is an article about a Hispanic American who made an important contribution to the United States. Think about how the information in this article adds to what you already know about Hispanic Americans. Remember to:

- Read the title to find out who or what the article is about.

- Read the introduction and headings to find out the main ideas of the article.

- Look for details to get additional facts. For example, ask yourself, "What did this person do to contribute to the space program?"

Important Contributor to the U.S. Space Program

Carlos Noriega, a Hispanic American, is a hero of America's space program.

Carlos Noriega, Astronaut

Astronaut Carlos Noriega was born in Lima, Peru, in 1959. He served as a Marine Corps pilot before he began to travel millions of miles beyond planet Earth. A mission specialist and computer scientist, Lieutenant Colonel Noriega helped assemble the International Space Station.

Main Idea _____

Details

- _____

- _____

- _____

Text Feature

Headings

When you read nonfiction, you need to know *What's this article about? What's the main idea here?* Here's how to figure it out.

Step 1 Read the title to find out what the article is about.

Step 2 Read the introduction to find out the main idea of the article.

Step 3 Read the headings to find out the main idea in each section.

Step 4 As you read, look for details to get additional facts.

Practice Your Skills!

1. Circle the sentence that tells the main idea of the article.

2. Check ✔ three details about what happens on the way to the lungs.

3. Underline the heading that tells what happens when air reaches the lungs.

PAIR SHARE What are the parts of the respiratory system?

How the Respiratory System Works

When you take a breath, all the parts of your respiratory system work together.

To the Lungs

❶ Air passes through the nose, nasal cavity, and windpipe on its way to the lungs.

❷ Air is warmed and cleaned in the nasal cavity.

❸ Air passes from the back of the nasal cavity into the windpipe.

❹ Bronchial (BRONG-kee-uhl) tubes take air from the windpipe to the two lungs.

In the Lungs

❺ When you breathe in, or **inhale**, your lungs take in oxygen. The oxygen then passes to your blood. When you breathe out, or **exhale**, your lungs put out carbon dioxide.

❻ In your lungs, the air moves into millions of tiny air sacs.

❼ Each air sac is surrounded by tiny vessels called capillaries. The capillaries take the oxygen from the air and send it into the blood.

❽ The capillaries also carry carbon dioxide from the blood to the lungs.

❾ Finally, carbon dioxide passes back out through the respiratory system when you breathe out.

NASAL CAVITY

WINDPIPE

BRONCHIAL TUBES

CAPILLARIES   AIR SACS

A Lifesaving Hug

A lifesaving technique, developed 30 years ago, is so important that it is taught in schools and posted in restaurants.

Heimlich Heroism

You're eating pizza at the mall. A friend starts to choke, cough, and gasp for air. Would you know what to do?

Carlos Barbosa, Jr., 7, of Rancho Cucamonga, California, did. The third-grader performed a lifesaving action called the **Heimlich maneuver** (HIME-lik muh-NOO-vir) after his dad began to choke on some baby carrots.

"I got behind my father and gave his stomach two squeezes," Carlos said. "The carrot popped out of his mouth and flew across the room."

Carlos had just learned about the lifesaving technique in *Scholastic News.* His class read about a student who used the Heimlich when his principal began choking on a piece of food in the school cafeteria.

Heimlich History

Henry Heimlich, an Ohio surgeon, developed the Heimlich maneuver. It **dislodges**, or removes, food that gets stuck in the throat and blocks breathing and speaking. Pressing the stomach forces air out of the lungs. The rush of air pushes out the food.

While it can save lives, the Heimlich maneuver can also be dangerous. If done improperly, it can break a person's ribs.

Each year, the American Red Cross teaches about 5 million Americas how to perform the Heimlich maneuver. Although Carlos had never practiced the move before, he did it correctly and saved his dad's life.

"I am lucky to have a son as smart as he is," said Carlos's grateful dad, Carlos Sr.

How to Heimlich

❶ Stand behind the person who is choking.

❷ Place the thumb side of one fist against the person's abdomen, or just slightly above the person's belly button.

❸ Hold your fist with your other hand. Press your fist into the person's belly. Use quick, upward presses. Repeat this process until food is dislodged.

❹ Once the food is out, the person should visit a doctor.

You can also do the Heimlich on yourself. Place one fist just over the belly button. Use the other hand to press upward.

REMEMBER: Seek training from an agency like the American Red Cross to learn the best, safest way to do the Heimlich maneuver.

On Your Own

Read the article below about the American Red Cross. Then use the information to complete the outline.

American Red Cross Helps Save Lives

The American Red Cross prepares people to save lives through health and safety education and training.

The American Red Cross offers courses that teach people lifesaving skills. This training is designed to give people the skills they need to respond in emergency situations. Courses include first aid, CPR, and Heimlich maneuver training.

Topic (who or what the article is about) _____

_____

Main Idea _____

_____

Details _____

_____

_____

Your school has many safety posters and instructions for what to do in an emergency. Look around your school and make a list of what you find.

_____   _____

_____   _____

_____   _____

Compare/Contrast

Before You Read

Vocabulary Read the sentences. Put a check mark to show if the statement is true or not.

What's the Word?

	YES	NO
A sad song about spring weather is a **carol**.		
You give a quick answer during a time of **reflection**.		
A time of **prosperity** is when you have everything you need.		
Always eating the same foods on a particular holiday is a **ritual**.		
Giving gifts on special holidays is a **tradition** for some families.		

As You Read

Text Structure This article compares and contrasts the way holidays are celebrated and why each is celebrated.

Text Feature How does keeping track of the main ideas and details help you understand the article and remember the information?

After You Read

1. What is the main idea of this article?

2. In what way are all the holidays similar?

3. Select two holidays. Compare and contrast why and how they are celebrated.

A Season of Celebration

The Holiday Season Highlights America's Diversity

For 30 days, Yasmeen Ahmed won't drink or eat until sunset. Yasmeen, 12, is a Muslim. She is fasting for Ramadan (RAH-muh-dahn), an Islamic holiday.

"When we fast, we can feel how the poor feel, and how hungry they are because they don't get to eat," says Yasmeen, who is from Bethlehem, Pennsylvania. She and her family also donate clothing and canned goods to the poor during Ramadan.

Americans practice different faiths—each with its own holidays. The freedom to practice religion is a major reason why the Pilgrims settled here.

During the last three months of the year, followers of many religions in America celebrate their holidays. The Muslim holiday Ramadan, the Hindu holiday Diwali (dih-WAH-lee), the Buddhist holiday Bodhi (BOH-dee) Day, the Jewish festival of Hanukkah (HAH-nuh-kuh), and the Christian holiday of Christmas are all celebrated in October, November, or December.

All in the Family

The story of Hanukkah reminds Jack Momeyer, 9, that miracles are all around him. "Hanukkah celebrates a miracle," says Jack, of New York City. "And I believe in miracles."

HANUKKAH: Candles are lit on each night.

RAMADAN: Lanterns are carried between homes.

DIWALI: The Hindu festival of lights is celebrated by placing clay oil lamps in each window and by lighting fireworks

Jack also loves being with his family to celebrate. "My grandfather comes over, and he sings the prayers out loud. My grandmother likes to make noodle pudding and matzo ball soup," says Jack. "I spin the dreidel (DRAY-duhl) with my big sister." A dreidel is a kind of spinning top.

Being with family also makes the holidays special for Delia Edner, 12, of Brooklyn, New York. "I love Christmas," Delia says. "We hang up stockings and fill them with candy." Delia also likes to sing Christmas carols.

A Time to Reflect

Some see the holidays as a time for reflection and prayer. Divya Singh, 14, who lives in Queens, New York, was born in India. "We pray for prosperity, knowledge, and peace," she says.

Alaina Hasegawa, 16, of Shoreline, Washington, reflects on the meaning of life on Bodhi Day. Bodhi Day celebrates enlightenment and the day when the founder of Buddhism became the Buddha, after meditating beneath a bodhi tree.

No matter what your beliefs are, age-old **rituals** and **traditions** have great meaning.

Paul Thayer, a religion and child expert, explains, "The rituals and traditions of holidays are fun and connect kids to the goodness of life."

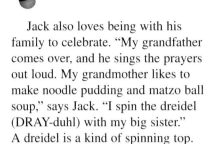

RELIGION	Christian	Muslim	Jewish	Buddhist	Hindu
HOLIDAY	Christmas December 25	Ramadan Month varies	Hanukkah December	Bodhi Day December 8	Diwali October or November
HOW THE HOLIDAY IS CELEBRATED	Many people go to church and most exchange gifts with family and friends.	Adult Muslims fast, or don't eat or drink, from dawn until sunset, and they feast during the twilight hours.	On each night of Hanukkah candles are lit on a menorah and family and friends exchange gifts.	Many Buddhists celebrate Bodhi Day with prayer and reflection.	Diwali is celebrated with a festival and by decorating the home with flowers and clay oil lamps.
WHY THE HOLIDAY IS CELEBRATED	Christmas is a joyful holiday that celebrates the birth of Jesus Christ.	Ramadan is a time to give thanks for the Koran, or sacred book of Islam.	It honors the miracle of one-day's oil supply keeping a temple lit for eight days.	Bodhi day celebrates when the religion's founder became enlightened.	Diwali honors the goddess of fortune and good luck.
PERCENTAGE OF U.S. POPULATION	76.5%	0.5%	1.3%	0.5%	0.4%

Compare/Contrast

Reread "A Season of Celebration." Fill in the graphic organizer by writing a check mark in each box that shows something that is done on the holiday shown at the top of the column. Then compare and contrast the holidays.

	Christmas	Ramadan	Hanukkah	Bodhi Day	Diwali
Pray					
Join family and friends					
Exchange gifts					
Sing songs and play games					
Joyful holiday					
Eat traditional foods					
Have a festival					
Candles or lights are part of the celebration					
Fast for part of the holiday					
Celebrates a person important to the religion					

Use the graphic organizer above to retell "A Season of Celebration" in your own words. Include as much information as you can remember.

Writing Frame

Use the information in your graphic organizer to fill in the writing frame.

Both Christmas and Hanukkah are similar in many ways. They are similar

because _____

_____

_____.

They are also similar because _____

_____.

However, in some ways, Christmas and Hanukkah are different. They are

different because _____

_____ and Hanukkah celebrates

_____.

So, _____ and _____

have both similarities and differences.

 Use the writing frame above as a model to compare and contrast two other festivals. For example, you may wish to compare and contrast a celebration held by a Native American group with a holiday you observe. Look in your social studies textbook if you need facts that will help you.

Text Feature

Maps

A **map** is a flat picture of all or part of Earth. Maps use symbols in addition to words. By doing this, maps can give you a lot of information in a limited space. Here's how to read a map.

Step 1 **Read the map title. It tells you what the map is about.** The map below shows where natural resources can be found in California.

Step 2 **Find the map symbols.** A symbol stands for a real thing or place. It may be a picture or a special color.

Step 3 **Look at the map key or legend. It tells what each map symbol means.** The symbols on this map represent California's natural resources. For example, the picture of a carrot represents vegetables.

Step 4 **Read the labels. These are important words to remember.** Each label tells the name of a geographic location. For example, Oakland is the name of a city in California.

Step 5 **Find the compass rose.** It shows directions on the map. **NW** stands for northwest, **SW** stands for southwest, **SE** stands for southeast, and **NE** stands for northeast.

Practice Your Skills!

1. Put an **X** on the name of the ocean that is west of California.

2. Circle the names of the two cities closest to the area where there are forests.

3. What natural resources are found near Los Angeles?

PAIR SHARE Do you think California is a good place to be a farmer? Why or why not? Use the map to support your answer.

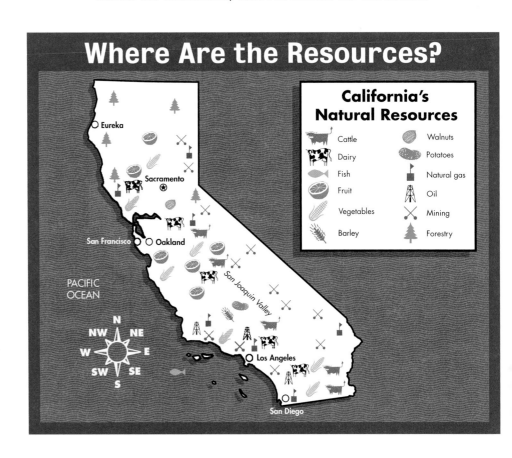

Where Are the Resources?

California's Natural Resources

Cattle	Walnuts
Dairy	Potatoes
Fish	Natural gas
Fruit	Oil
Vegetables	Mining
Barley	Forestry

Eureka

Sacramento

San Francisco   Oakland

San Joaquin Valley

PACIFIC OCEAN

Los Angeles

San Diego

N
NW   NE
W   E
SW   SE
S

Amazon Mapmakers

Brazil's Rain Forests

Amazon children check out a rain forest map that their tribe helped to create.

Rain forests are one of the planet's most difficult environments to map. That hasn't stopped Amazon Indians from mapping 10 million acres of Brazil's rain forest.

The new map is the most detailed map of the Amazon rain forest ever made. The map covers an area of the rain forest that is slightly larger than the state of Maryland.

Several groups, including four Amazon Indian tribes, worked together on the project. The groups learned how to use mapping tools and how to collect data. They set out to cover every square inch of the territories in which they live.

The map includes mountains and rivers. It also includes the Amazon peoples' **cultural** landmarks, such as fishing and hunting grounds that their ancestors (AN-ses-ters) have used for millions of years. "What looks to us like an empty forest is [to the Amazon people] full of wealth and meaning," says Vasco van Roosmalen, director of the mapping project. "The Indians know these forests like we know the insides of our houses, but the problem has always been that the knowledge has never been recorded."

The Amazon people are using the map to teach children about their rich history and culture.

On Your Own

This map of Brazil has a special purpose. It tells about the weather in that country on a typical day in January, which is summer south of the Equator. Think about how the information in this map adds to what you already know about Brazil. Remember to:

- Read the map's title and labels.

- Study the map carefully.

- Think about the information it shows. For example, ask yourself, "In Brazil, what kind of weather is usual during January?"

WEATHER MAP OF BRAZIL JANUARY 29

 Write three questions about the map. When you're done, change papers with a partner. Answer each other's questions.

1._____

2._____

3._____

Maps

A **map** is a flat picture of all or part of Earth. Maps use symbols in addition to words. By doing this, maps can give you a lot of information in a limited space. Here's how to read a map.

Step 1   **Read the map title. It tells you what the map is about.** The map below shows South America.

Step 2   **Find the map symbols.** A symbol stands for a real thing or place. It may be a picture or a special color.

Step 3   **Look at the map key or legend.** It tells what each map symbol means.

Step 4   **Read the labels.** Labels tell names of countries, rivers, mountains, oceans, and other geographical places.

Step 5   **Find the compass rose.** It shows directions on the map.

Step 6   **Find the locator.** The locator is a small map set on the main map. It shows where the area of the main map is located.

Rain Forests of South America

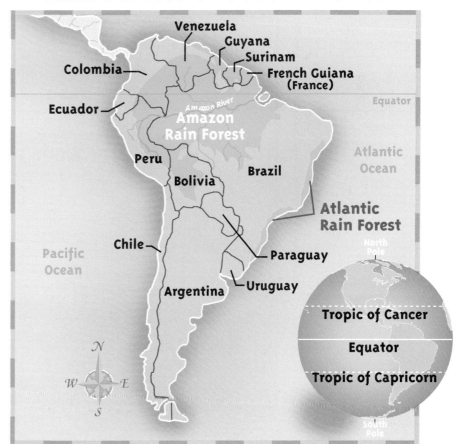

Practice Your Skills!

1. Put an **X** on the country in which the Amazon Rain Forest is located.

2. Circle the name of the ocean closest to the Atlantic Rain Forest.

3. Which rain forest is closest to the Equator?

PAIR SHARE   How would you compare and contrast the sizes and locations of the two rain forests shown on the map?

Saving the Wilderness

Before You Read

Preview the article. Check (✔) the special features it has.

_____ title
_____ headings
_____ labels
_____ symbols
_____ map
_____ caption
_____ photo
_____ boldfaced words

As You Read

• Did you read the title of the map?
❏ Yes ❏ No

• Did you read the map key?
❏ Yes ❏ No

• Did you find the compass rose on the map?
❏ Yes ❏ No

• Explain what you learned from reading the map.

After You Read

1. How would you describe wilderness areas?

2. What does *biodiversity* mean?

PAIR SHARE Tell why scientists are interested in saving wilderness areas.

What Is Wilderness?

According to a recent study, wilderness is defined as a land area comprising at least 3,861 square miles. The area must also contain no more than 13 people per square mile. On top of that, it must still have at least 70 percent of its original plants and trees.

What do you think of when you hear the word "wilderness"? Do you picture a distant, windswept prairie, or a jungle teeming with giant, exotic plants?

Do you think of wilderness as a thing of the past? If so, here's news that may surprise you! A recent study found that nearly half of the Earth's land area is still wilderness.

The study found 37 wilderness areas around the world (see map below). The areas include woodlands, tropical rain forests, deserts, wetlands, tundra, and **boreal,** or northern, forests.

Why Save the Wilderness?

Scientists named 5 of the 37 wilderness regions as "high-priority" areas for conservation. These regions

Many different kinds of animals and plants live in rain forests.

have the highest **biodiversity,** or the greatest variety of plants and animals.

"These wilderness areas are critical to the survival of the planet," says scientist Russell Mittermeier, who helped with the study. "They help regulate weather patterns and rainfall and are major storehouses for biodiversity."

The World's Wilderness

Arctic Tundra

Arctic Tundra

Boreal Forest

Boreal Forest

Pacific Coastal Forests

Northern Rocky Mountains

European Mountains

Central Asian Deserts

Mojave Desert

Colorado Plateau

Appalachian Mountains

Sahara/Sahel

Arabian Deserts

Sundarbans (Ganges Delta)

The Sonoran and Baja California Deserts

Chihuahuan Desert

Llanos

Congo Forests of Central Africa

New Guinea

0° Equator

Amazonia

Sudd

Serengeti Plain

Arnhem Land

N

Coastal Deserts of Peru and Chile

Pantanal

Caatinga

Namib Desert

Miombo-Mopane Woodlands and Grasslands

The Kimberly

Australian Deserts

Cape York Peninsula

Gran Chaco

Bañados del Este

Kalahari

Okavango

Tasmania

Magellanic Subpolar Rain Forests

Patagonia

KEY ▪ High-priority areas

Antarctica

On Your Own

Below is a map of the United States. Think about the information it shows. For example, ask yourself, "Are there wilderness areas in every state?"

Wilderness Areas in the U.S.

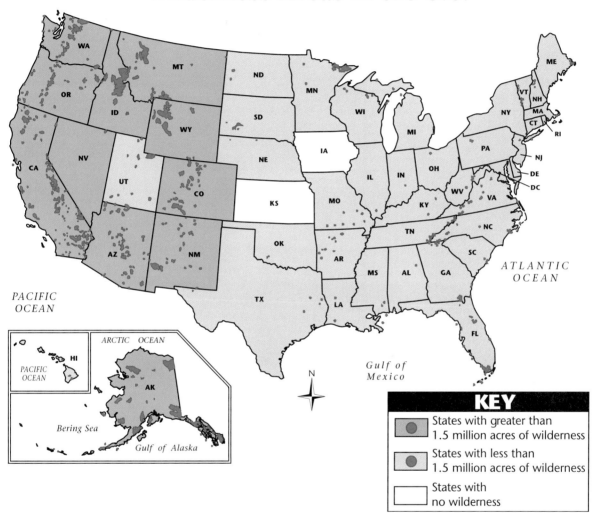

KEY

- States with greater than 1.5 million acres of wilderness
- States with less than 1.5 million acres of wilderness
- States with no wilderness

YOU BE THE EXPERT!

Write three questions that can be answered by the map. Then, change papers with a partner. Answer each other's questions.

1. _____

2. _____

3. _____

Description

Practice Your Skills!

Before You Read

Vocabulary Read the words below. Then check the column that shows what each word describes.

Words That Describe

	Where	Weather
aboveground		
scorching		
heat		
underground		
cool		
down under		
desert		

As You Read

Text Structure This article describes some unique homes of people who live in different parts of the world. To keep track of them do the following: (1) underline words that name and describe the homes; (2) circle the words that tell in which country the home is built.

Text Feature How does the map help you understand the article?

After You Read

1. Why were these homes built?

2. Study the map. Which of the countries mentioned in the text is surrounded by water?

3. Which of these unique homes could you make where you live? Why?

California (U.S.)

Pacific Ocean

AUSTRALIA

This dugout eating area probably looks similar to the eating area in your home.

Down Under

In Coober Pedy, Australia, people really live "down under." In this opal-mining town, nearly half of the residents live in dugouts, or homes that people dug into the sides of hills. Coober Pedy is in the desert, and living underground helps them stay cool. Dugouts are just like homes aboveground, where other families live.

No Place Like Home

TURKEY
ASIA
TUNISIA
SYRIA
AFRICA
Atlantic Ocean
Indian Ocean

People around the world live in all kinds of structures that you might not think of as traditional homes. Some are built out of necessity as protection from harsh climates. Others were built for protection from enemies.

All Natural

In Syria, some villagers top their houses with natural materials to get relief from the heat. Builders pour layers of wet mud onto the tops of houses. Villagers allow the mud to dry as layers of mud hang over each other, forming a big cone roof. More mud plaster is added for a smooth finish to give these homes their beehive shape. The mud keeps the cool in and the heat out.

In the African country of Tunisia, some people live underground and use a ladder to reach their home. For more than 700 years, some people here have kept cool in the scorching desert by digging out pits, or holes in the ground. Residents carve a central courtyard underground, then continue to carve through rock to add rooms to a home. Rock is a great barrier (BARE-ee-ur) against heat and wind.

Solid as a Rock

In Turkey, these towers of rocks are known as "fairy chimneys." Thousands of years ago, a volcano spread lava all over the area of Cappadocia (cap-uh-DOE-shuh). Wind and water helped shape the hard lava into cones. People dug holes, and set up their homes inside. About 6,000 years ago, the first residents found that these homes protected them against invaders. Today, about 1,000 people in one village still call these chimneys home.

The people who first built these homes had good reasons for building them the way they did.

Description

Reread "No Place Like Home." Fill in the graphic organizer with details that describe each of the homes.

Unique Homes			
Kind of Home	Location	How Built	Advantages of Home

 Use the graphic organizer above to retell "No Place Like Home" in your own words. Include as much information as you can remember.

Writing Frame

Use the information in your graphic organizer to write a summary of the article.

Unusual homes have been built all over the world. In Australia, some people

live in _____ .

These homes _____ .

People like them because _____ .

In Tunisia, some people live in _____ .

These homes _____ .

The advantage of these homes is that _____ .

In Turkey, some people live in _____ .

These homes _____ .

Years ago, people found that this was a good kind of home because _____

_____ .

In Syria, some people live in _____ .

These homes are good because _____ .

_____ .

 Use the writing frame above as a model to write a description of unique homes that can be found in other parts of the world such as the pueblos in the Southwest United States or the yurts, also known as *gers*, in Mongolia.

Flow Charts

Some nonfiction explains a process. The article often includes a flow chart. A **flow chart** is a kind of diagram that shows a sequence of steps in the order they happen. It helps you "picture" the information. Here's how to read a flow chart.

Step 1 Read the title to find out what the flow chart is about.

Step 2 Follow the numbers to read the steps in order.

Step 3 Study the illustration for each step. Read the label and explanation carefully.

Practice Your Skills!

1. Draw a line from Step **2** to the part of the flow chart it describes.

2. Circle the labels that name the materials used to make glass.

3. What is the last step in the process?

PAIR SHARE Explain in your own words how glass bottles are made.

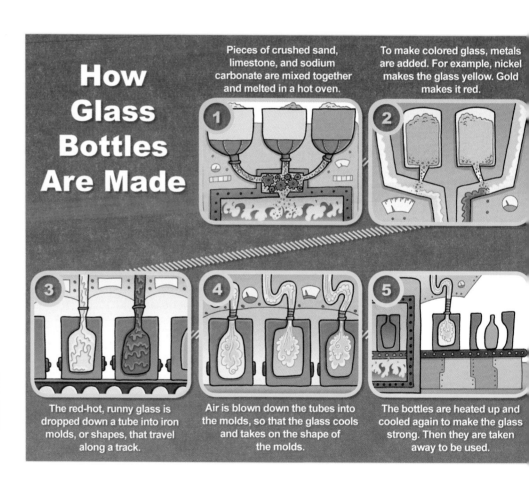

How Glass Bottles Are Made

1 Pieces of crushed sand, limestone, and sodium carbonate are mixed together and melted in a hot oven.

2 To make colored glass, metals are added. For example, nickel makes the glass yellow. Gold makes it red.

3 The red-hot, runny glass is dropped down a tube into iron molds, or shapes, that travel along a track.

4 Air is blown down the tubes into the molds, so that the glass cools and takes on the shape of the molds.

5 The bottles are heated up and cooled again to make the glass strong. Then they are taken away to be used.

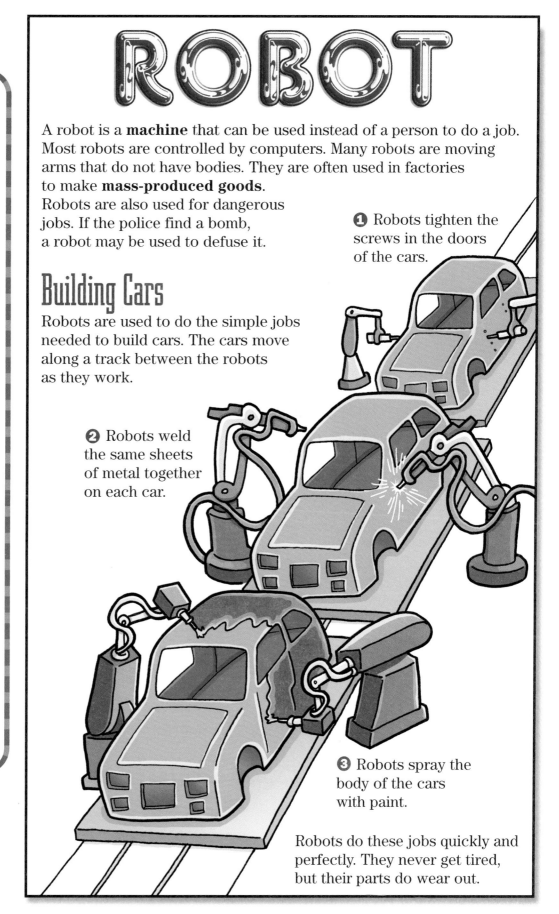

Practice Your Skills!

Before You Read

Preview the article. Check (✔) the special features it has.

_____ title
_____ introduction
_____ headings
_____ flow chart
_____ numbered steps
_____ captions
_____ illustrations
_____ boldfaced words

As You Read

- Did you read the title to find out the topic?
  ❏ Yes ❏ No

- Did you read each step in order?
  ❏ Yes ❏ No

- Did you connect each step to a part of the picture?
  ❏ Yes ❏ No

- Explain how you read the flow chart.

After You Read

1. What three jobs can robots do to build cars?

2. What are mass-produced goods?

PAIR SHARE What are some benefits of using robots?

ROBOT

A robot is a **machine** that can be used instead of a person to do a job. Most robots are controlled by computers. Many robots are moving arms that do not have bodies. They are often used in factories to make **mass-produced goods**. Robots are also used for dangerous jobs. If the police find a bomb, a robot may be used to defuse it.

Building Cars

Robots are used to do the simple jobs needed to build cars. The cars move along a track between the robots as they work.

❶ Robots tighten the screws in the doors of the cars.

❷ Robots weld the same sheets of metal together on each car.

❸ Robots spray the body of the cars with paint.

Robots do these jobs quickly and perfectly. They never get tired, but their parts do wear out.

On Your Own

Below is a flow chart showing how crayons are made. Think about the information it shows. For example, ask yourself, "What is the order of the steps needed to make a crayon?"

How Crayons Are Made

1. Crayons are made from wax and pigment, which is a powdered coloring material. Pigment is added to hot wax and mixed.

2. The mixture is poured into crayon-shaped molds, which are then cooled.

3. The crayons are removed from the molds and inspected. Crayons that are not perfect are put aside.

4. A special machine glues a label onto each crayon.

5. The crayons are packed in boxes.

Write three questions that can be answered by the flow chart. When you're done, change papers with a partner. Answer each other's questions.

1. _____

2. _____

3. _____

LESSON 26

Text Feature

Flow Charts

In science, you read about all kinds of cycles, such as the life cycle. A cycle can be pictured in a flow chart. A **flow chart** is a kind of diagram that shows a sequence of steps in the order they happen. Some flow charts go around and around. That's because they show a cycle that doesn't end. It goes on and on over time.

Step 1 **Read the title and introduction to find out what the flow chart is about.** The flow chart below shows how an underwater food web happens.

Step 2 **Use the numbers and arrows to follow the steps in their correct order.** Start with number 1.

Step 3 **Study each picture and read the explanation.** The explanation is in or near the part of the flow chart it describes.

Step 4 **Be sure you understand what happens in each step.** Go back and forth between the picture and the explanation.

Practice Your Skills!

1. Circle the word that tells what some sea animals eat before they die.

2. Put an **X** on the sentence that tells what happens after dead sea animals get covered in mud.

3. Why does this flow chart go around and around?

PAIR SHARE In the ocean, how are plants and animals dependent on one another?

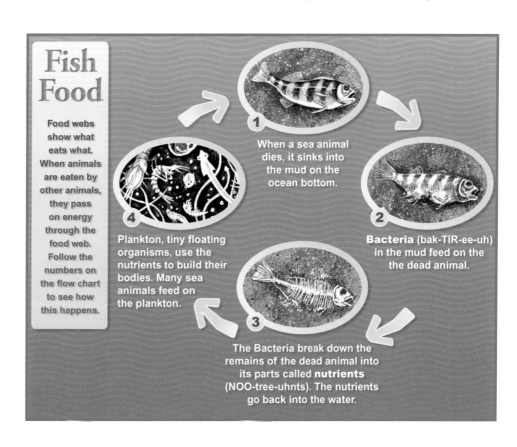

Fish Food

Food webs show what eats what. When animals are eaten by other animals, they pass on energy through the food web. Follow the numbers on the flow chart to see how this happens.

1. When a sea animal dies, it sinks into the mud on the ocean bottom.

2. **Bacteria** (bak-TIR-ee-uh) in the mud feed on the the dead animal.

3. The Bacteria break down the remains of the dead animal into its parts called **nutrients** (NOO-tree-uhnts). The nutrients go back into the water.

4. Plankton, tiny floating organisms, use the nutrients to build their bodies. Many sea animals feed on the plankton.

Before You Read

Preview the article. Check (✔) the special features it has.

_____ title
_____ labels
_____ flow chart
_____ arrows
_____ numbers
_____ illustrations
_____ pronunciations
_____ boldfaced words

As You Read

• Do you know what the boldfaced words mean?
❏ Yes ❏ No

• Did you read the flow chart title to find out the topic?
❏ Yes ❏ No

• Did you follow the arrows?
❏ Yes ❏ No

• Explain how you read the flow chart.

After You Read

1. What do some ocean animals eat?

2. What is another word for _hunter?_

PAIR SHARE How do ocean animals depend on each other for survival?

What Feeds What?

Ocean animals depend on each other for survival. Some eat plants. Others hunt and eat other animals. These hunters are called **predators**. The animals that they hunt and eat are called **prey** (pronounced "pray"). Most predators are also prey for other, bigger animals. Predators that aren't eaten by other animals are called top predators.

A **food web** shows what feeds what. Follow the arrows from the prey to its predators.

Ocean Prey and Predators

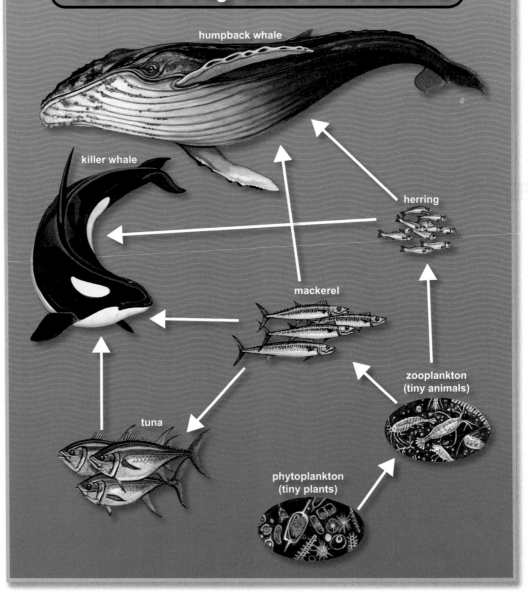

humpback whale

killer whale

herring

mackerel

zooplankton (tiny animals)

tuna

phytoplankton (tiny plants)

On Your Own

Read the article below about the food web. Then complete the flow chart to show the information discussed in the text. Include a number for each part and arrows to show the sequence, or order, of the food web.

THE FOOD WEB

This food web is made up of four main parts. The first part is the sun. The sun provides energy for everything on our planet.

The next part of the food web consists of producers. Green plants are producers. They use energy from the sun to produce oxygen and food that all organisms need in order to live.

Consumers are the third part of the food web. Consumers are every organism that eats something else. These include plant-eating animals, animals that eat other animals, scavengers that eat dead animals, and parasites that live off of other organisms.

The last part of the food web is made up of decomposers, such as fungi and bacteria. They convert dead matter into gases that are released back into the air, soil, or water. They recycle the nutrients to be used again by plants, the producers.

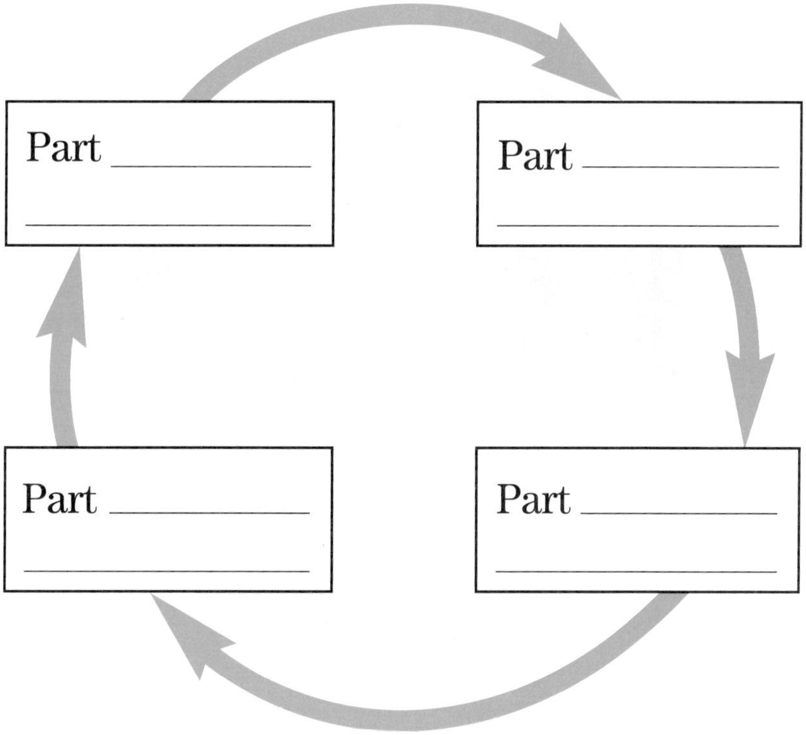

Part _____
_____

Part _____
_____

Part _____
_____

Part _____
_____

Cause/Effect

Practice Your Skills!

Before You Read

Vocabulary Read each word. Then put a check in the column that shows what you know about it.

Knowledge Rating Chart

	climate	evaporation	vapor	precipitation	zone
I can define it.					
I know something about it.					
I don't know it.					

As You Read

Text Structure This article gives information about how rain forms. It includes facts about the **causes** and the **effects** in this cycle. You will see that in the rain cycle, an effect then becomes the cause of the next step. To find an effect, ask yourself, "What happened?" To find the cause, ask yourself, "Why did this happen?"

Text Feature How does the flow chart help you understand how rain forms?

After You Read

1. Why is the sun important in causing rain?

2. Study the flow chart. What would happen if there were no cool air?

3. What are the steps in the rain cycle?

Weather and Climate

Will it rain at tomorrow's baseball game?

How hot will it be at the beach? Will there be enough wind to fly a kite this afternoon? All these questions are about weather, something that affects our lives every day.

The place we live in usually has the same pattern of weather over a longer period of time. It may have hot, dry weather in summer and warm, wet weather in winter. This usual, or average, pattern of weather over a longer period of time is called **climate**. What's the climate where you live?

Average Yearly Rainfall in U.S. Cities

CITY	RAINFALL (in inches)	CITY	RAINFALL (in inches)
Albuquerque, NM	9	Boston, MA	43
San Francisco, CA	20	Portland, OR	36
Honolulu, HI	18	Reno, NV	8
Cleveland, OH	37	Los Angeles, CA	13
Houston, TX	46	Savannah, GA	49
Lander, WY	13	Little Rock, AK	51
New Orleans, LA	64	Miami, FL	58

Source: *World Almanac 2003*
National Climate Data Center

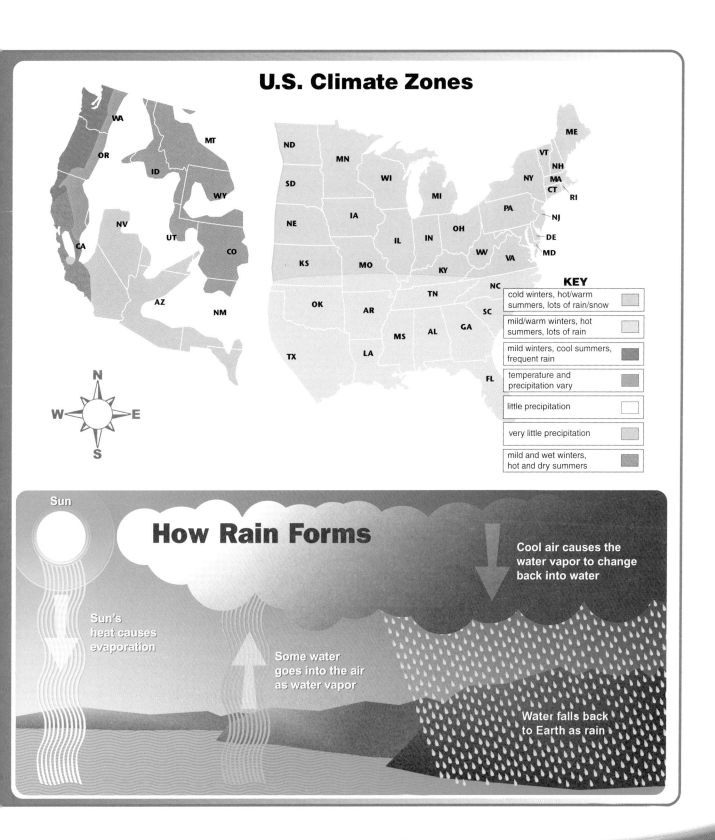

U.S. Climate Zones

KEY

cold winters, hot/warm summers, lots of rain/snow	
mild/warm winters, hot summers, lots of rain	
mild winters, cool summers, frequent rain	
temperature and precipitation vary	
little precipitation	
very little precipitation	
mild and wet winters, hot and dry summers	

How Rain Forms

Sun

Sun's heat causes evaporation

Some water goes into the air as water vapor

Cool air causes the water vapor to change back into water

Water falls back to Earth as rain

Cause/Effect

Reread "Weather and Climate." Look carefully again at the cycle flow chart, "How Rain Forms." Fill in the cause/effect chart to show the causes and effects that lead to rain.

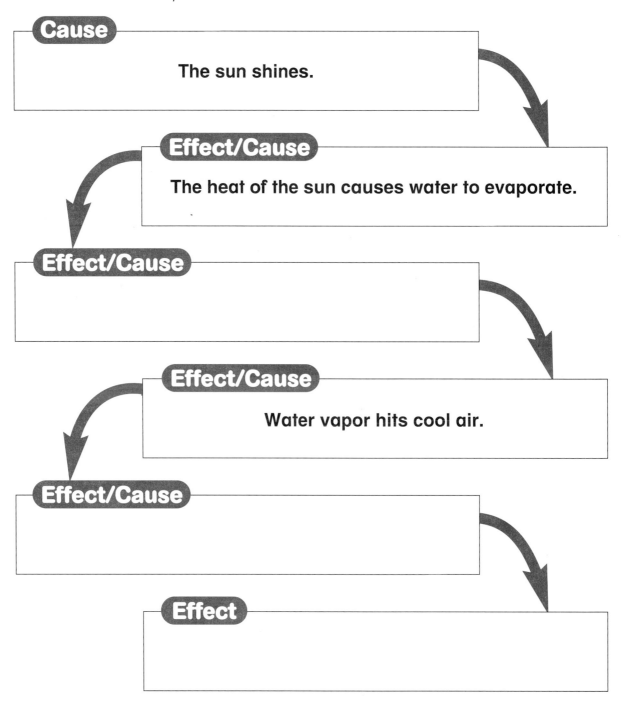

Cause

The sun shines.

Effect/Cause

The heat of the sun causes water to evaporate.

Effect/Cause

Effect/Cause

Water vapor hits cool air.

Effect/Cause

Effect

Use the graphic organizer above to retell "Weather and Climate" in your own words. Include as much information as you can remember.

Writing Frame

Use the information in your graphic organizer to fill in the writing frame.

This is how rain forms.

The heat of the sun _____

_____

_____ .

Because of evaporation, _____

_____ .

When water vapor hits cool air, it causes _____

_____ .

As a result, _____

_____ .

This explains how rain forms.

 Use the writing frame above as a model to describe another example of cause/effect, such as how we hear or how electricity flows through a circuit. Look in your science textbook if you need facts that will help you fill in the frame.

Primary Sources

A **primary source** is an original source giving information about a person or event in history. A primary source is an account of an event told by a person who was present at the event. It often includes the person's feelings about what happened. A primary source can make you feel like you were there. Photographs, quotes, letters, speeches, diaries, and artifacts are also primary sources. Here's how to read an article with primary sources.

Step 1 **Read the title to find out what the article is about.** The title of the article below tells us about life on the Oregon Trail.

Step 2 **Preview the text to learn about the topic. Look for any primary source material.** The article below includes a primary source—a diary entry written in 1849.

Step 3 **Read the primary source material. Pay attention to who wrote it and when.** Ask yourself how the information in the diary adds to what you already know about pioneer life.

Practice Your Skills!

1. Put an **X** on the name of the place where Sallie's family camped.

2. Circle the names of the foods that the family had.

3. How did the pioneers protect themselves at night?

PAIR SHARE How would you describe life on the Oregon Trail?

Life on the Oregon Trail: Sallie Hester

One way we know about the pioneers is from the diaries they kept. A diary is a written record of what someone has done or thought each day. Read the following words from a diary written by a 14-year-old girl named Sallie Hester.

Diary written by Sallie Hester, May 21, 1849

Camped on the beautiful Blue River with plenty of wood and good grazing for our cattle. Our family all in good health. We had two deaths in our train within the past week of cholera (KAHL-ur-uh). When we camp at night, we form a corral with our wagons. We sleep in our wagons on feather beds. We live on bacon, ham, rice, dried fruits, molasses, packed butter, bread, coffee. Occasionally, some of the men kill an antelope and then we have a feast; and sometimes we have fish on Sunday.

THE OREGON TRAIL

Practice Your Skills!

Before You Read

Preview the article. Check (✔) the special features it has.

_____ title
_____ headings
_____ map
_____ photos
_____ primary sources
_____ date
_____ captions
_____ boldfaced words

As You Read

- Did you read the title of the article?
  ❏ Yes ❏ No

- Did you read the headings?
  ❏ Yes ❏ No

- Did you find the primary sources?
  ❏ Yes ❏ No

- Explain how you read the article.

After You Read

1. How did Rebecca Ketchum feel about the prairie?

2. Why did people decide to travel west?

PAIR SHARE Why might people have traveled west in large groups of wagons? Would you enjoy traveling west during this time period? Why or why not?

These people built new homes in the West.

THE BEGINNING OF THE TRAIL

In the 1840s, groups of people traveled west on the Oregon Trail. These people were looking for better lives and new homes. They became pioneers.

Many people from different places came to Independence, Missouri. Independence is where the Oregon Trail begins. Sometimes 100 wagons traveled together.

This trail marker was on the Oregon Trail.

"The prairie, oh the broad, the beautiful, the **bounding** [hilly] rolling **prairie**! Imagine the ocean, when the waves are rolling mountains high, becoming solid and covered with beautiful green grass and you have some faint idea of it."

—*Rebecca Ketchum, 1853*

THE END OF THE TRAIL

Out West, many people found land to farm. They cleared the land, planted crops, and built homes.

On Your Own

Below is a description of St Louis, Missouri, a city where many pioneers came to prepare for their trip west. Imagine that you and your family are preparing for a journey on the Oregon Trail. Use the information below to create a diary entry you might write.

- Write a date for your diary entry

- Tell what the town looks like and what you and your family did on that day.

- Tell how you feel as you prepare for your trip. For example, what are you happy about or what are you afraid of?

St. Louis, 1845

On April 16, 1845, the town of St. Louis was jammed with thousands of people preparing for their trip on the Oregon Trail. People were buying what they needed for the trip in the many shops lining the streets. There were wagon repair shops and places to get new shoes for horses. There were food stores and stores selling tools.

A family of four needed to store more than a thousand pounds of food for the journey. They bought bacon, flour, coffee, sugar, and salt for their trip. They loaded their food onto farm wagons. These wagons, which had covers to keep out the dust and rain, were often overloaded by the time the families set out.

Everyone was waiting for late April or early May. They waited for the grass to grow because if the pioneers headed west too early, the grass wouldn't be long enough for their animals to graze.

My Diary

Date _____

_____

_____

_____

_____

_____

_____

_____

_____

_____

_____

_____

_____

Text Feature

Primary Sources

A **primary source** can be an account of an event by someone who witnessed it. For example, a quotation from someone "on the scene" can tell you about what happened and how the person felt about it.

Step 1 **Read the title to find out what the article is about.** The article is about a Native American, John Herrington, and makes us wonder why he is called "Rocket Man."

Step 2 **Preview the text to learn about the topic. Look for any primary source material.** These may include quotations, interviews and photographs.

Step 3 **Read the main article, then the primary source material.** Sometimes the primary source material is in the article. Sometimes it's set off in a sidebar.

Rocket Man
JOHN HERRINGTON, CHICKASAW

Astronaut John Herrington sure is reaching for the stars. He recently became the first Native American ever to go to space.

Herrington, who is a Chickasaw, blasted off to the International Space Station (ISS). The ISS is a station where scientists live and work on space experiments. While there, Herrington performed three spacewalks to install, or put in, new equipment.

To make this historic trip even more special, Herrington brought a few objects on the spacecraft to honor his people. They included a Chickasaw flag, eagle feathers, and two arrowheads.

Chickasaw John Herrington performing one of his spacewalks.

When John Herrington was selected for an astronaut spot, he said the following: "Anything's possible. There is a great amount of responsibility. It can motivate people. They can realize their dreams can come true."

Practice Your Skills!

1. Put an **X** on the name of the first Native American to work in space.

2. (Circle) the objects Herrington brought on the spacecraft.

3. Underline the words that tell what Herrington did in space.

PAIR SHARE What did you learn about John Herrington from his quotation?

Practice Your Skills!

Preview the article. Check (✔) the special features it has.

_____ title
_____ quotations
_____ map
_____ photo
_____ headings
_____ questions
_____ caption
_____ boldfaced words

As You Read

- Did you read the title of the article?
  ❏ Yes ❏ No

- Did you preview the article, looking for primary sources?
  ❏ Yes ❏ No

- Did you study the primary source material?
  ❏ Yes ❏ No

- Explain what you found out by reading the article.

After You Read

1. Who was Ellen Ochoa's role model and why?

2. What does Ellen Ochoa say about astronaut training?

 PAIR SHARE What advice does Ellen Ochoa give to young people who would like to become astronauts?

Students interviewed Ellen Ochoa, the first Hispanic-American woman to fly in space. Here are excerpts from that interview.

Ellen Ochoa is the first Hispanic-American woman to fly into space.

Q: Does your being Hispanic American make you feel more pressure and more pride about your accomplishments?

A: I don't believe that being Hispanic American puts any additional pressure on me. I seem to put enough pressure on myself. As for my accomplishments, being an astronaut has given me the opportunity to speak to children all over, including children with the same background as myself. I think that it's important for children to have a role model, someone whose example they can follow, so they can see what they can grow up to be. It's important they know that if they work hard, they can be and accomplish whatever they want. I am proud to be an example of that.

Q: Who do you think was the most influential person in your life?

A: My mother influenced (in-FLU-inst) me the most. When I was a year old, she started college. She had to raise five children primarily on her own, so she couldn't take more than one class each semester. She didn't graduate until 22 years later, but she did finish. Her primary focus was the enjoyment of learning. That's what I got from her example.

Q: What is NASA training like?

A: Everything is always harder to do in training. In training, we prepare for anything that could happen on a space mission—anything that could go wrong. In training things keep breaking, problems have to be solved. Nothing has ever gone wrong on any of my trips into space, and our training helps us make sure that nothing will. For my last mission, we trained for nine months before the actual flight. I started my formal NASA training in 1990. During that period I spent about half my time in training. The other half I spent performing other duties. I was in training for three years before my first mission, which isn't that long of a wait. Some astronauts have waited 10, even 16 years before they finally go into space!

Q: I love math and I want to become an astronaut. What can I start to do to prepare myself?

A: It's good you love math, because in order to be an astronaut, a college degree in math or a technical science is very important. Being an astronaut isn't just science, though. An astronaut must be both a team player and a leader. You should get involved in activities where you work closely with other people because working closely with other people is an essential part of being an astronaut! There are many things you can do that could help you in learning to work with people—playing on a sports team, for instance, or learning a musical instrument and being in a band or an orchestra.

On Your Own

Below is an outline for an interview. Think of someone you'd like to interview about the work they do. For example, you might want to interview someone who delivers mail or someone who works with young children. Fill in the interview outline by writing the questions you'd ask and the answers the person might give.

- Write a title for your interview.

- Include an introduction that tells what kind of work the person does.

- Include questions about what the person needs to know and advice they have for people who might want to do the same kind of work.

An Interview With _____

Introduction _____ is a person who _____
_____.

Question 1_____
_____.

Answer _____
_____
_____.

Question 2_____
_____.

Answer _____
_____
_____.

Question 3_____
_____.

Answer _____
_____
_____.

Question 4_____
_____.

Answer _____
_____
_____.

Sequence

Before You Read

Vocabulary Here are some important words from the article. Think about each word's meaning. Then fill in the chart.

expedition   mission   wildlife

What's the Connection?

Words	Synonyms	Related Words Why?
journey expedition	Yes ☐ No ☐	Yes ☐ No ☐ Why?
mission permission	Yes ☐ No ☐	Yes ☐ No ☐ Why?
wildlife wildfire	Yes ☐ No ☐	Yes ☐ No ☐ Why?

As You Read

Text Structure This article tells about Lewis and Clark's journey to explore the land west of the Mississippi River. As you read, underline the date that the trip began. Pay attention to the sequence of events.

Text Feature How do the pictures of primary sources and quotations help you understand the article?

After You Read

1. Which facts show that Thomas Jefferson was a curious man?

2. Study the map. What does it show?

3. Did Jefferson make a wise choice in choosing Lewis to head the expedition? Why or why not?

OFF TO ADVENTURE:

In Lewis and Clark's time, little was known about the land west of the Mississippi River. They were sent to explore the **region**. Today, this area is the Northwestern United States. The article below explains how their trip began. Now, pretend it is May 14, 1804 . . .

Jefferson Orders Expedition

For years, President Thomas Jefferson has wondered what kinds of unusual plants and animals exist west of the Mississippi River. He has also wanted to learn more about the people living in that area. And there's one more reason he called for this trip.

Last year, in 1803, the United States doubled in size. That's because the United States bought the Louisiana Territory from France (see map). This new land must be explored and mapped. Jefferson chose Meriwether Lewis to lead the big mission.

Into the Wild

Lewis, a former U.S. Army officer, has worked as President Jefferson's secretary, or assistant. He's spent a lot of time in the wild, and knows how to study animals and plants. He will report on all the wildlife in the region.

Lewis knew he'd need help on this job. One of the first things he did was to ask his old Army captain, William Clark, to join him. Clark has also spent much time in the wild and is skilled in making maps.

Lewis included sketches of plants and animals in his journal

Lewis and Clark

Leading a team of almost 50 other explorers, Lewis and Clark set out today on the Missouri (mi-ZUR-ee) River. They will travel by boat, foot, and on horseback across thousands of miles. What will they find? Even they don't know.

The explorers don't even know how long the mission will last. It will probably take several years!

Lewis and Clark will keep journals of their adventures. We'll be able to read about their discoveries once they return!

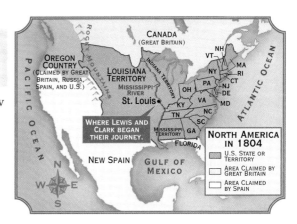

NORTH AMERICA IN 1804
- U.S. STATE OR TERRITORY
- AREA CLAIMED BY GREAT BRITAIN
- AREA CLAIMED BY SPAIN

DOG OF DISCOVERY

Not every member of the Lewis and Clark team is human. Seaman, a big black Newfoundland dog owned by Lewis, is also along for the trip.

Seaman will be valuable, or very important, to the team. During his time with Lewis, he has proved to be a good hunter. He is skilled at catching squirrels for his owner.

"I thought the squirrels, when fried, to be a pleasant food," Lewis said.

During the journey, Seaman will serve on guard duty each night. If strangers or wild animals approach the team members as they sleep, Seaman will bark a warning.

Lewis is not the only one who values Seaman. Some Shawnee people recently wanted to buy the dog from Lewis.

"One Shawnee offered me three beaver skins for my dog," said Lewis. "But I prize my dog too much, so of course there was no deal."

Newfoundland dogs are strong and good swimmers. Their fur is thick, so dogs do not soak up much water.

TOOLS FOR THE TRIP

Before Meriwether Lewis, William Clark, and their team could begin their journey, they needed a lot of equipment. Lewis gathered about 4,000 pounds of goods to be taken on the trip!

What's needed for such an adventure? The team is bringing 193 pounds of a thick paste made of eggs, vegetables, and beef. (This paste turns into soup when heated!) To hunt, they are carrying rifles and knives. The team also has 150 yards of cloth to be sewn into tents and sheets. To help them find their way, they have the latest, most advanced devices for explorers. They will use telescopes and compasses, or instruments for finding directions.

The explorers have also brought gifts for the American Indians they expect to meet on their journey. The gifts include mirrors, ivory combs, sewing needles, scissors, face paint, ribbons, and colored beads.

Lewis and Clark used a pocket compass like this one to help them find their way. Compasses have a magnetic needle that always points north.

Sequence

Reread "Off to Adventure." Fill in the graphic organizer to show the order in which the events listed below happened.

- Lewis and Clark set out with a team of almost 50 explorers.
- Jefferson orders a journey to explore the land west of the Mississippi.
- Lewis chooses Clark to be his assistant.
- The United States buys the Louisiana Territory.
- Jefferson chooses Lewis to lead the expedition.

Exploring the Louisiana Territory

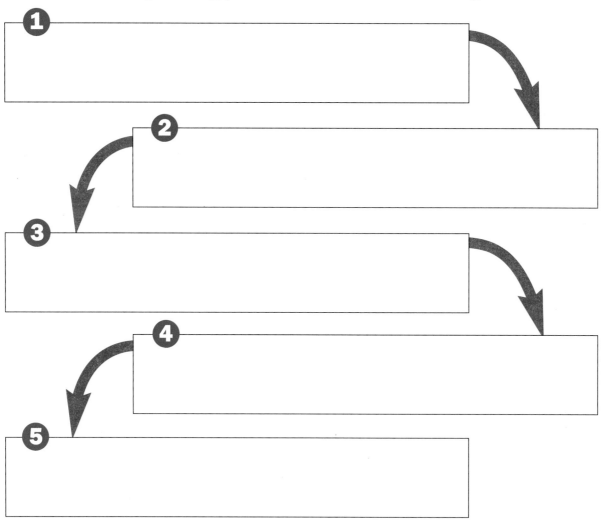

 Use the graphic organizer above to retell "Off to Adventure" in your own words. Remember to tell the events in the order in which they happened.

Writing Frame

Use the information in your graphic organizer to fill in the writing frame.

The United States purchased the Louisiana Territory from France. The first

thing President Thomas Jefferson did was to _____

_____

_____ .

After that, he chose Lewis to _____

_____ .

Next, Lewis chose _____

_____ .

He chose him because _____

_____ .

Finally, on May 14, 1804, _____

_____ .

 Use the writing frame above as a model to write about the sequence of events that led to another expedition in history. Look in your social studies textbook if you need facts that will help you fill in the frame.

LET'S NAVIGATE

Follow the five easy steps when you read nonfiction text.

5 EASY STEPS

Step ① Preview
Read the title, introduction, and headings. Think about what they tell you.

Step ② Prepare
Say to yourself, "This article is going to be about _____. What do I already know?"

Step ③ Read
Carefully read the article.

Step ④ Use the Tools
Stop at special features, such as the special type and the graphics. Ask yourself,

- Why is this here?
- What does it tell me?
- How does it connect to the article?

Step ⑤ Retell/Connect
Retell what you learned. Think about how it connects to your life and the world.

① # THE AMAZING OCTOPUS

The octopus is an awesome ocean animal. It can be as HUGE as 30 feet or as tiny as 1 inch in length. What makes this creature so amazing?

Body Parts

③ An octopus has 8 arms that it uses to swim and to catch food. An octopus has suction cups on the back of its arms.

④ **Suction cups** help the octopus grab a meal, such as crabs, clams, and fish. If an octopus loses an arm, it can grow another one. This is called **regeneration** (ree-gen-uh-RAY-shun). A starfish can do the same thing.

An octopus has no bones, so its body is soft and squishy. This allows it to squeeze into small spaces. An octopus can squeeze into a seashell! This helps the octopus chase food even into little cracks.

Survival Skills ②

Octopuses have many ways to avoid their enemies. An octopus can change colors as **camouflage** (KAM-uh-flahzh), a way to blend in with its surroundings. That way, its enemies can't see it. And, in the blink of an eye, it can make its skin bumpy. To an enemy, the octopus looks like just another rock!

An octopus can also squirt purple-black ink at its enemies. The enemy can't see the octopus through the ink, and the octopus can quickly swim away to safety.

⑤

TEXT STRUCTURES

Cause/ Effect

cause

effect

Problem/ Solution

problem

solution

Sequence

step 1 step 2 step 3 step 4

Description

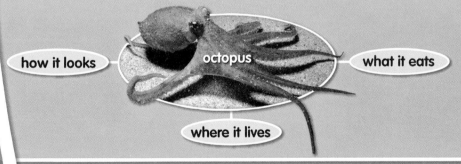

how it looks octopus what it eats

where it lives

Compare/ Contrast

land animals both water animals

Sequence

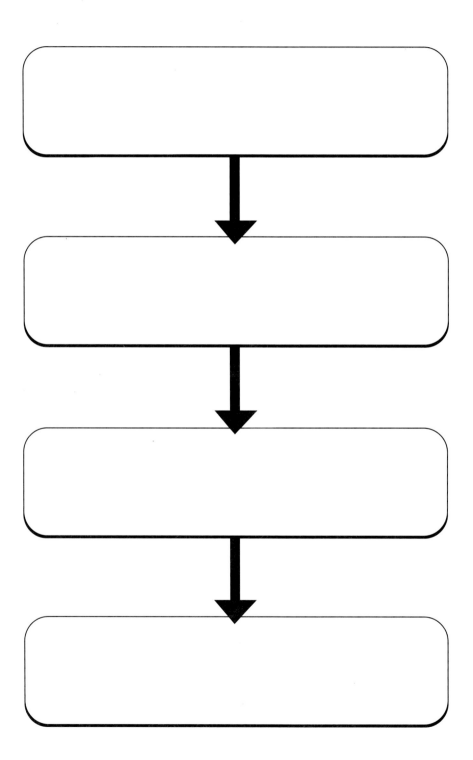

Compare/Contrast

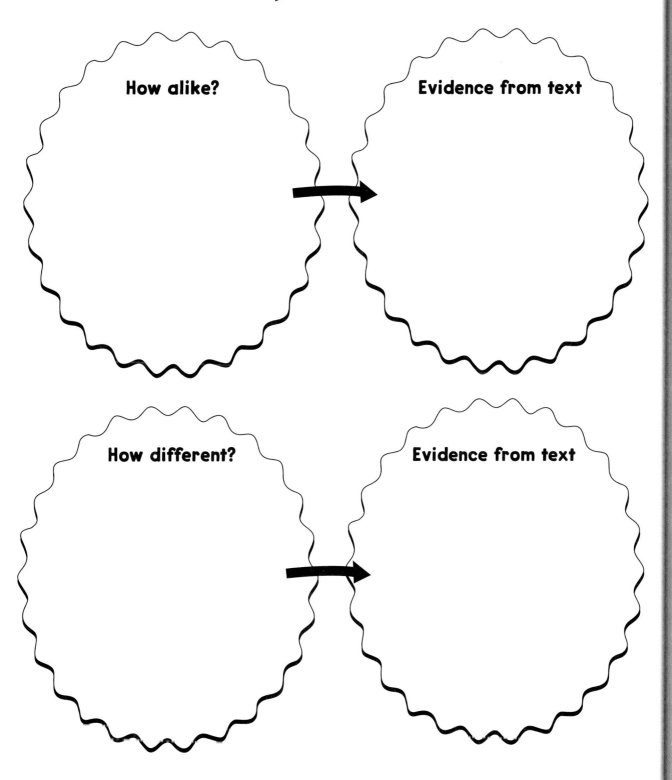

How alike?

Evidence from text

How different?

Evidence from text

Cause/Effect

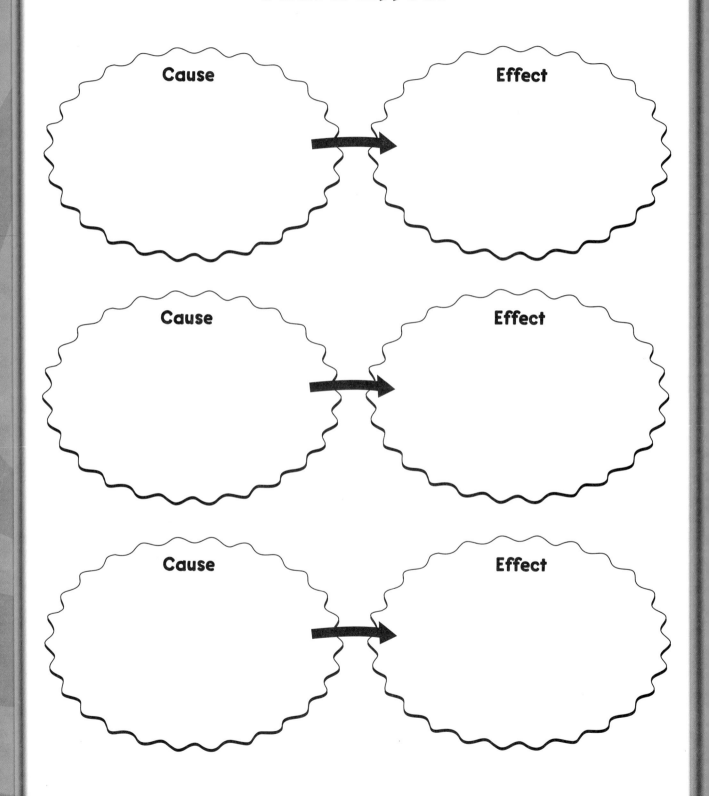

Cause   **Effect**

Cause   **Effect**

Cause   **Effect**

Problem/Solution

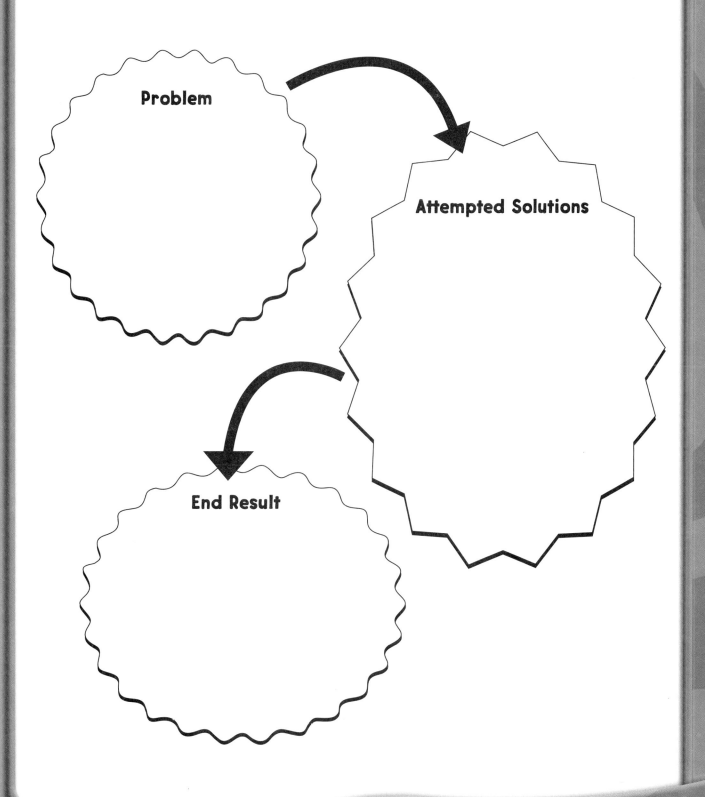

Problem

Attempted Solutions

End Result

Description

Main Idea _____

_____

Detail 1 _____

_____

Detail 2 _____

_____

Detail 3 _____

_____

Detail 4 _____

_____

Credits

Text: ""Hip Hoppers," "National Parks," "Protect Our Parks," "A Long Winter's Nap," "Their Idea of Fun," "Straw Dreams," "Eating for Energy," "Have Fun! Get Healthy!", "Honoring Martin Luther King, Jr.," "Flying Through History," "A Handy Way to Stay Healthy," "Germ Hangouts," "A People Place," "Thirsty Land," "Jeffrey Pine Bark," "Help for Howlers," "37 Million and Growing," "A Lifesaving Hug," "How to Heimlich," "A Season of Celebration," "Where Are the Resources," "Amazon Mapmakers," "Saving the Wilderness," "No Place Like Home," "Rocket Man," and "Off to Adventure" are reprinted from SCHOLASTIC NEWS. Copyright © 2000, 2001, 2002, 2003, 2004 by Scholastic Inc. Reprinted by permission. "Cool Critters," "Snow Monkeys," "Wild About Winter," "Arctic Hares," and "Could Your Body Go to Mars?" are reprinted from SUPER SCIENCE. Copyright © 2001, 2002, 2005 by Scholastic Inc. Reprinted by permission. "A Race Across Alaska," "Celebrate Hispanic Heritage," and "An Interview With Ellen Ochoa" are reprinted from www.scholastic.com. Copyright © 2006–1996. Reprinted by permission. "Coming to America" is reprinted from TEACHING STUDENTS TO READ NONFICTION. Copyright © 2003 by Alice Boynton and Wiley Blevins, published by Scholastic Inc. Reprinted by permission. "Forests on Fire" is reprinted from SCIENCE PLACE. Copyright © Scholastic Inc. Reprinted by permission. "Life on the Oregon Trail: Sallie Hester" is reprinted from COMMUNITIES: ADVENTURES IN TIME AND SPACE. Copyright © 1997 by Macmillan/McGraw-Hill. Reprinted by permission. "How Glass Bottles Are Made" and "Robot" are reprinted from HOW THINGS WORK. Copyright © Scholastic Inc. Reprinted by permission. "What Goes on a Food Label," "The Oregon Trail," and "Coming to Hawaii" are reprinted from CONTENT AREA READING: SOCIAL STUDIES. Copyright © Scholastic Inc. Reprinted by permission. "How the Respiratory System Works" is reprinted from CONTENT AREA READING: SCIENCE. Copyright © Scholastic Inc. Reprinted by permission.

Images: Cover: Skater © Royalty-Free/Corbis; Mexican Dancers © Tony Anderson/Getty Images; Astronaut © Adastra/Getty Images; Sea Turtle © Tobias Berhard/Jupiter Images. Page 4: Robert & Linda Mitchell. Page 5: (clockwise, from top) R. Mickens/AMNH; Michael & Patricia Fogden/Minden Pictures; Blake Sheldon/Animals Animals; Joe McDonald/Clyde Peeling's Reptiland/AMNH. Page 7: Brian LaRossa. Page 8: © W. Perry Conway/Corbis. Page 9: Brian LaRossa. Page 10: Tom Walker/Photo Researchers. Page 11: (from left) Ken M. Highfill/Photo Researchers; Stephen J. Lang/Visuals Unlimited. Page 14: AP Photo/Al Grillo. Page 15: (from top) © Rex Rysted; Courtesy Aniak Volunteer Fire Department; Brian LaRossa. Page 16: © John Conrad/Corbis. Page 17: Tim Laman/National Geographic Image Collection. Page 18: (from top) Johnny Johnson/Getty Images; Norbert Rosing/National Geographic Image Collection. Page 19: John Dunn/Arctic Light/National Geographic Image Collection. Page 20: Cheryl Humbert. Page 21: (clockwise, from top left) Mapman/Scholastic; © 2002 Harpo Productions, Inc. Photo by George Burns. All rights reserved; Red Feather Development Group; Cheryl Humbert. Page 25: (clockwise, from top left) Stephen Stickler/Getty Images; © Photodisc Royalty-Free; (lettuce, broccoli, orange) © Photodisc Royalty-Free; (milk, fish) Copyright © 2007 Scholastic and its licensors. All rights reserved. Page 27: (maps) Brian LaRossa; (illustrations) Teresa Southwell. Page 28: (clockwise, from top right) © Corbis; © 2003 PhotoSpin, Inc. (map) Brian LaRossa; (illustrations) Teresa Southwell. Page 29: Brian LaRossa. Page 30: © Photodisc Royalty-Free. Page 31: © Photodisc Royalty-Free. Page 34: © Bettmann/Corbis. Page 35: (from top) NOAA; © North Wind Picture Archives; © The Granger Collection, New York; NOAA; NASA. Page 36: NOAA. Page 37: Photo by Francis Miller/Time Life Pictures/Getty Images. Page 38: © The Granger Collection, New York. Page 39: © Bettmann/Corbis. Page 40: (clockwise, from top left) Orville Wright & John T. Daniel/KRT; Lennox McLendon/AP Wide World; (2) AP Wide World. Page 41: (top) Marvin Fong/The Plain Dealer/AP Wide World, Reuters; (clockwise, from left) AP Wide World; NASA; Charles Whitehouse/AP Wide World; NASA. Page 47: Michelle Kwajafa/Morguefile.com. Page 48: © Bettmann/Corbis. Page 51: Ron Barrett. Page 54: 5W Infographic. Page 55: (from left) © Frans Lanting/Corbis; Ryan Sias. Page 56–59: Teresa Southwell. Page 60: (from left) Stone; Robert Winslow/Animals Animals. Page 61: (from left) Nathan Hale; Tim Fitzharris/Minden Pictures. Page 64: Photodisc via SODA. Page 65: (from top) AP Photo; SODA; © David Atlas/Retna Ltd. Page 66: NASA. Page 67: Brian LaRossa. Page 68: (from top) Barbara Grover; Courtesy of the American Red Cross. Page 69: Brian LaRossa. Page 70: (from left) Bushnell/Soifer/Stone; Nabir/AFP/Corbis; Joe Viesti. Page 74: Brian LaRossa. Page 75: (from left) Amazon Conservation Team; Mapman/Scholastic; (background) emlyn@morquefile.com. Page 76: Brian LaRossa; Page 77: Mapman/Scholastic. Page 78: (from top) © Kevin Schafer/Corbis; Brian LaRossa. Page 79: Brian LaRossa. Page 80: (from top) Chad Slattery; Mapman/Scholastic;

Editor: Mela Ottaiano
Cover Design: Jorge J. Namerow